NEW PERSPECTIVES ON
HTML and CSS
6th Edition

BRIEF

Patrick Carey

COURSE TECHNOLOGY
CENGAGE Learning

Australia • Brazil • Japan • Korea • Mexico • Singapore • Spain • United Kingdom • United States

COURSE TECHNOLOGY
CENGAGE Learning™

New Perspectives on HTML and CSS, 6th Edition, Brief

Vice President, Publisher: Nicole Jones Pinard

Executive Editor: Marie L. Lee

Associate Acquisitions Editor: Amanda Lyons

Senior Product Manager: Kathy Finnegan

Product Manager: Leigh Hefferon

Associate Product Manager: Julia Leroux-Lindsey

Editorial Assistant: Jacqueline Lacaire

Director of Marketing: Elisa Roberts

Senior Marketing Manager: Ryan DeGrote

Marketing Coordinator: Kristen Panciocco

Developmental Editor: Sasha Vodnik

Content Project Manager: Jennifer Goguen McGrail

Composition: GEX Publishing Services

Art Director: Marissa Falco

Text Designer: Althea Chen

Cover Designer: Roycroft Design

Cover Art: © Veer Incorporated

Copyeditor: Suzanne Huizenga

Proofreader: Kathy Orrino

Indexer: Alexandra Nickerson

© 2012 Course Technology, Cengage Learning

ALL RIGHTS RESERVED. No part of this work covered by the copyright herein may be reproduced, transmitted, stored or used in any form or by any means graphic, electronic, or mechanical, including but not limited to photocopying, recording, scanning, digitizing, taping, Web distribution, information networks, or information storage and retrieval systems, except as permitted under Section 107 or 108 of the 1976 United States Copyright Act, without the prior written permission of the publisher.

For product information and technology assistance, contact us at
Cengage Learning Customer & Sales Support, 1-800-354-9706
For permission to use material from this text or product, submit all requests online at **www.cengage.com/permissions**
Further permissions questions can be emailed to
permissionrequest@cengage.com

Some of the product names and company names used in this book have been used for identification purposes only and may be trademarks or registered trademarks of their respective manufacturers and sellers.

Microsoft and the Office logo are either registered trademarks or trademarks of Microsoft Corporation in the United States and/or other countries. Course Technology, Cengage Learning is an independent entity from the Microsoft Corporation, and not affiliated with Microsoft in any manner.

Disclaimer: Any fictional data related to persons or companies or URLs used throughout this book is intended for instructional purposes only. At the time this book was printed, any such data was fictional and not belonging to any real persons or companies.

Library of Congress Control Number: 2010943381

ISBN-13: 978-1-111-52645-0

ISBN-10: 1-111-52645-1

Course Technology
20 Channel Center Street
Boston, MA 02210
USA

Cengage Learning is a leading provider of customized learning solutions with office locations around the globe, including Singapore, the United Kingdom, Australia, Mexico, Brazil, and Japan. Locate your local office at:
international.cengage.com/global

Cengage Learning products are represented in Canada by Nelson Education, Ltd.

To learn more about Course Technology, visit **www.cengage.com/course technology**

To learn more about Cengage Learning, visit **www.cengage.com**

Purchase any of our products at your local college store or at our preferred online store
www.cengagebrain.com

Printed in the United States of America
1 2 3 4 5 6 7 8 9 15 14 13 12 11

Preface

The New Perspectives Series' critical-thinking, problem-solving approach is the ideal way to prepare students to transcend point-and-click skills and take advantage of all that HTML and CSS have to offer.

In developing the New Perspectives Series, our goal was to create books that give students the software concepts and practical skills they need to succeed beyond the classroom. We've updated our proven case-based pedagogy with more practical content to make learning skills more meaningful to students. With the New Perspectives Series, students understand *why* they are learning *what* they are learning, and are fully prepared to apply their skills to real-life situations.

"I love this text because it provides detailed instructions and real-world application examples. It is ideal for classroom and online instruction. At the end of the term my students comment on how much they've learned and put to use outside the classroom."

—Bernice Howard
St. Johns River Community
College

About This Book

This book provides essential coverage of HTML and CSS, and includes the following:
- Up-to-date coverage of using HTML5 and XHTML to create Web sites
- Instruction on accessing CSS style sheets and JavaScript programs, storyboarding complete Web sites, and creating and applying client-side image maps
- Reinforcement of code compliance with HTML and XHTML syntax

New for this edition!
- Each session begins with a Visual Overview, which includes colorful, enlarged figures with numerous callouts and key term definitions, giving students a comprehensive preview of the topics covered in the session, as well as a handy study guide.
- New ProSkills boxes provide guidance for how to use the software in real-world, professional situations, and related ProSkills exercises integrate the technology skills students learn with one or more of the following soft skills: decision making, problem solving, teamwork, verbal communication, and written communication.
- Important steps are highlighted in yellow with attached margin notes to help students pay close attention to completing the steps correctly and avoid time-consuming rework.

System Requirements

This book assumes that students have an Internet connection, a text editor, and a current browser that supports HTML5 and CSS3. The following is a list of the most recent versions of the major browsers at the time this text was published: Internet Explorer 9 (public beta), Firefox 4.0.2 (public beta), Safari 5.0.2, Opera 10.6, and Google Chrome (6.04). More recent versions may have come out since the publication of this book. Students should go to the Web browser home page to download the most current version. All browsers interpret HTML and CSS code in slightly different ways. It is highly recommended that students have several different browsers installed on their systems for comparison. Students might also want to run older versions of these browsers to highlight compatibility issues. The screenshots in this book were produced using Internet Explorer 9.0 running on Windows 7 Professional (64-bit), unless otherwise noted. If students are using different browsers or operating systems, their screens will vary slightly from those shown in the book; this should not present any problems in completing the tutorials.

www.cengage.com/ct/newperspectives

The New Perspectives Approach

VISUAL OVERVIEW

PROSKILLS

KEY STEP

INSIGHT

TIP

REVIEW

APPLY

REFERENCE

GLOSSARY/INDEX

Context

Each tutorial begins with a problem presented in a "real-world" case that is meaningful to students. The case sets the scene to help students understand what they will do in the tutorial.

Hands-on Approach

Each tutorial is divided into manageable sessions that combine reading and hands-on, step-by-step work. Colorful screenshots help guide students through the steps. **Trouble?** tips anticipate common mistakes or problems to help students stay on track and continue with the tutorial.

Visual Overviews

New for this edition! Each session begins with a Visual Overview, a new two-page spread that includes colorful, enlarged figures with numerous callouts and key term definitions, giving students a comprehensive preview of the topics covered in the session, as well as a handy study guide.

ProSkills Boxes and Exercises

New for this edition! ProSkills boxes provide guidance for how to use the software in real-world, professional situations, and related ProSkills exercises integrate the technology skills students learn with one or more of the following soft skills: decision making, problem solving, teamwork, verbal communication, and written communication.

Key Steps

New for this edition! Important steps are highlighted in yellow with attached margin notes to help students pay close attention to completing the steps correctly and avoid time-consuming rework.

InSight Boxes

InSight boxes offer expert advice and best practices to help students achieve a deeper understanding of the concepts behind the software features and skills.

Margin Tips

Margin Tips provide helpful hints and shortcuts for more efficient use of the software. The Tips appear in the margin at key points throughout each tutorial, giving students extra information when and where they need it.

Assessment

Retention is a key component to learning. At the end of each session, a series of Quick Check questions helps students test their understanding of the material before moving on. Engaging end-of-tutorial Review Assignments and Case Problems have always been a hallmark feature of the New Perspectives Series. Colorful bars and brief descriptions accompany the exercises, making it easy to understand both the goal and level of challenge a particular assignment holds.

Reference

Within each tutorial, Reference boxes appear before a set of steps to provide a succinct summary and preview of how to perform a task. In addition, each book includes a combination Glossary/Index to promote easy reference of material.

www.cengage.com/ct/newperspectives

Our Complete System of Instruction

Coverage To Meet Your Needs

Whether you're looking for just a small amount of coverage or enough to fill a semester-long class, we can provide you with a textbook that meets your needs.

- Brief books typically cover the essential skills in just 2 to 4 tutorials.
- Introductory books build and expand on those skills and contain an average of 5 to 8 tutorials.
- Comprehensive books are great for a full-semester class, and contain 9 to 12+ tutorials.

So if the book you're holding does not provide the right amount of coverage for you, there's probably another offering available. Go to our Web site or contact your Course Technology sales representative to find out what else we offer.

CourseCasts – Learning on the Go. Always available…always relevant.

Want to keep up with the latest technology trends relevant to you? Visit our site to find a library of podcasts, CourseCasts, featuring a "CourseCast of the Week," and download them to your mp3 player at http://coursecasts.course.com.

Our fast-paced world is driven by technology. You know because you're an active participant—always on the go, always keeping up with technological trends, and always learning new ways to embrace technology to power your life.

Ken Baldauf, host of CourseCasts, is a faculty member of the Florida State University Computer Science Department where he is responsible for teaching technology classes to thousands of FSU students each year. Ken is an expert in the latest technology trends; he gathers and sorts through the most pertinent news and information for CourseCasts so your students can spend their time enjoying technology, rather than trying to figure it out. Open or close your lecture with a discussion based on the latest CourseCast.

Visit us at http://coursecasts.course.com to learn on the go!

Instructor Resources

We offer more than just a book. We have all the tools you need to enhance your lectures, check students' work, and generate exams in a new, easier-to-use and completely revised package. This book's Instructor's Manual, ExamView testbank, PowerPoint presentations, data files, solution files, figure files, and a sample syllabus are all available on a single CD-ROM or for downloading at http://www.cengage.com/coursetechnology.

Content for Online Learning

Course Technology has partnered with the leading distance learning solution providers and class-management platforms today. To access this material, visit www.cengage.com/webtutor and search for your title. Instructor resources include the following: additional case projects, sample syllabi, PowerPoint presentations, and more. For students to access this material, they must have purchased a WebTutor PIN-code specific to this title and your campus platform. The resources for students might include (based on instructor preferences): topic reviews, review questions, practice tests, and more. For additional information, please contact your sales representative.

SAM: Skills Assessment Manager

SAM is designed to help bring students from the classroom to the real world. It allows students to train and test on important computer skills in an active, hands-on environment.

SAM's easy-to-use system includes powerful interactive exams, training, and projects on the most commonly used Microsoft Office applications. SAM simulates the Office application environment, allowing students to demonstrate their knowledge and think through the skills by performing real-world tasks, such as bolding text or setting up slide transitions. Add in live-in-the-application projects, and students are on their way to truly learning and applying skills to business-centric documents.

Designed to be used with the New Perspectives Series, SAM includes handy page references, so students can print helpful study guides that match the New Perspectives textbooks used in class. For instructors, SAM also includes robust scheduling and reporting features.

Acknowledgments

I would like to thank the people who worked so hard to make this book possible. Special thanks to my developmental editor, Sasha Vodnik, for his hard work and valuable insights, and to my Product Manager, Kathy Finnegan, who has worked tirelessly in overseeing this project and made my task so much easier with her enthusiasm and good humor. Other people at Course Technology who deserve credit are Marie Lee, Executive Editor; Julia Leroux-Lindsey, Associate Product Manager; Jacqueline Lacaire, Editorial Assistant; Jennifer Goguen McGrail, Senior Content Project Manager; Christian Kunciw, Manuscript Quality Assurance (MQA) Supervisor; and John Freitas, Susan Pedicini, and Danielle Shaw, MQA testers.

Feedback is an important part of writing any book, and thanks go to the following reviewers for their helpful ideas and comments: Bernice Howard, St. Johns River Community College; Lisa Macon, Valencia Community College; Sharon Scollard, Mohawk College; Luke Sui, Daytona State College; and John Taylor, Southeastern Technical College.

I want to thank my wife Joan and my six children for their love, encouragement and patience in putting up with a sometimes distracted husband and father. This book is dedicated to the memory of Mac Mendelsohn, who generously gave me my chance in this business and whose constant encouragement in the early years inspired me and taught me so much.
– Patrick Carey

TABLE OF CONTENTS

TUTORIAL 1

OBJECTIVES

Session 1.1
- Explore the history of the Internet, the Web, and HTML
- Compare the different versions of HTML
- Study the syntax of HTML tags and attributes
- Define a Web page head, body, and title
- Work with the HTML5 structural elements

Session 1.2
- Mark page headings, paragraphs, block quotes, and addresses
- Create unordered and ordered lists
- Apply an external style sheet to a Web page
- Run a JavaScript program
- Mark text-level elements including strong and emphasized text
- Insert inline images and line breaks
- Insert special characters from extended character sets

Getting Started with HTML5

Creating a Product Page for a Small Business

Case | *The J-Prop Shop*

Dave Vinet owns a small business called the J-Prop Shop that builds and sells circus props and equipment. Dave is looking to expand his business and his visibility by upgrading his Web site. Dave has already written the text for the Web site's home page and has generated some of the graphic images for it. He has come to you for help in designing a Web page and writing the code. Dave hopes to build on his Web page in the future as his business expands, so he would like you to write code that takes advantage of the latest Web standards, including HTML5. Your job will be to create a sample home page that Dave can use as a foundation for his new Web site.

STARTING DATA FILES

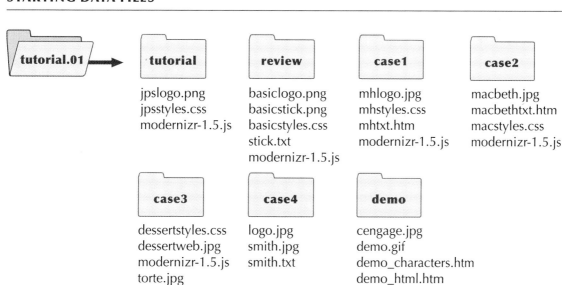

tutorial.01 →

tutorial
jpslogo.png
jpsstyles.css
modernizr-1.5.js

review
basiclogo.png
basicstick.png
basicstyles.css
stick.txt
modernizr-1.5.js

case1
mhlogo.jpg
mhstyles.css
mhtxt.htm
modernizr-1.5.js

case2
macbeth.jpg
macbethtxt.htm
macstyles.css
modernizr-1.5.js

case3
dessertstyles.css
dessertweb.jpg
modernizr-1.5.js
torte.jpg
tortetxt.htm

case4
logo.jpg
smith.jpg
smith.txt

demo
cengage.jpg
demo.gif
demo_characters.htm
demo_html.htm
demo2.gif
modernizr-1.5.js

SESSION 1.1 VISUAL OVERVIEW

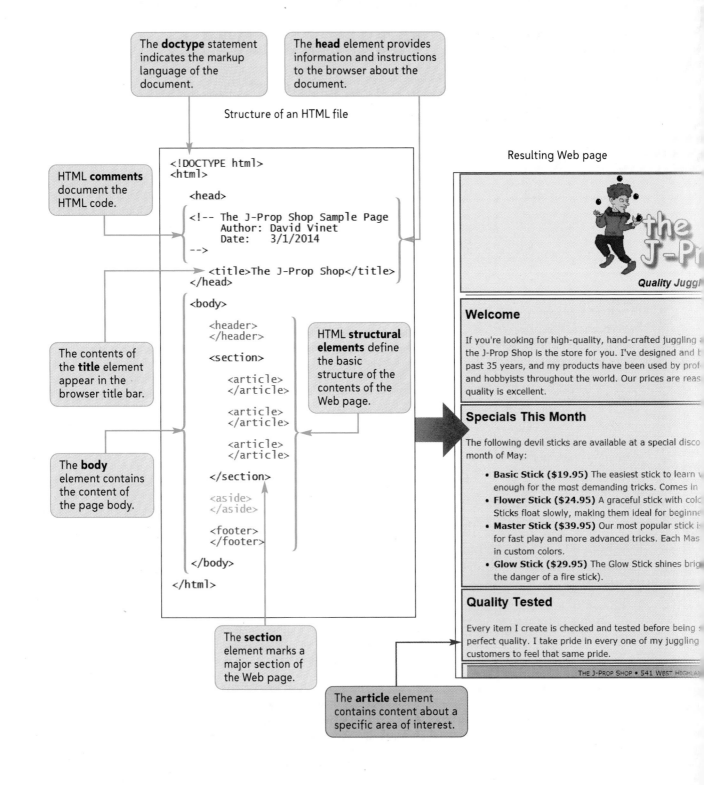

The **doctype** statement indicates the markup language of the document.

The **head** element provides information and instructions to the browser about the document.

Structure of an HTML file

Resulting Web page

HTML **comments** document the HTML code.

```
<!DOCTYPE html>
<html>

    <head>

    <!-- The J-Prop Shop Sample Page
         Author: David Vinet
         Date:   3/1/2014
    -->

        <title>The J-Prop Shop</title>
    </head>

    <body>

        <header>
        </header>

        <section>

            <article>
            </article>

            <article>
            </article>

            <article>
            </article>

        </section>

        <aside>
        </aside>

        <footer>
        </footer>

    </body>

</html>
```

The contents of the **title** element appear in the browser title bar.

The **body** element contains the content of the page body.

HTML **structural elements** define the basic structure of the contents of the Web page.

The **section** element marks a major section of the Web page.

The **article** element contains content about a specific area of interest.

Welcome

If you're looking for high-quality, hand-crafted juggling a the J-Prop Shop is the store for you. I've designed and h past 35 years, and my products have been used by prof and hobbyists throughout the world. Our prices are reas quality is excellent.

Specials This Month

The following devil sticks are available at a special disco month of May:

- **Basic Stick ($19.95)** The easiest stick to learn v enough for the most demanding tricks. Comes in
- **Flower Stick ($24.95)** A graceful stick with colo Sticks float slowly, making them ideal for beginne
- **Master Stick ($39.95)** Our most popular stick i for fast play and more advanced tricks. Each Mas in custom colors.
- **Glow Stick ($29.95)** The Glow Stick shines brig the danger of a fire stick).

Quality Tested

Every item I create is checked and tested before being perfect quality. I take pride in every one of my juggling customers to feel that same pride.

Quality Juggl

THE J-PROP SHOP • 541 WEST HIGHLA

THE STRUCTURE OF AN HTML5 DOCUMENT

The **head**er element contains an introduction to the page.

Markup Tags

Document elements are marked using **tags**.

```
<h2>Welcome</h2>
<p>If you're looking for high-
   juggling and circus product
   the store for you. I've des
   for the past 35 years, and
   used by professional entert
   throughout the world. Our p
   our quality is excellent.
</p>
```

Resulting Web page

Welcome

If you're looking for high-quali
the J-Prop Shop is the store fo
past 35 years, and my produc
and hobbyists throughout the
quality is excellent.

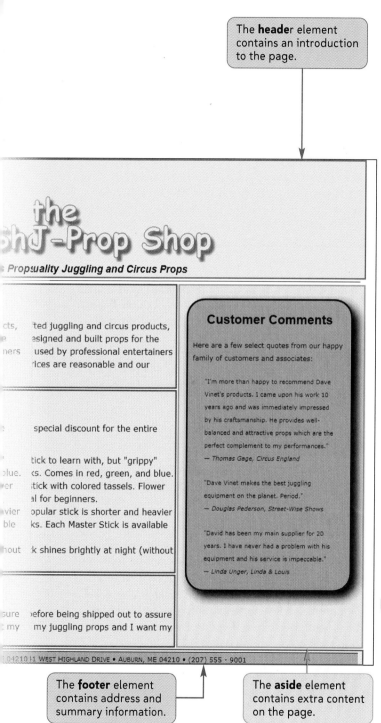

Two-sided tags mark elements that contain textual content or other elements

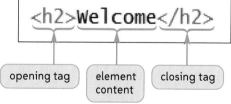

```
<h2>Welcome</h2>
```

opening tag   element content   closing tag

One-sided tags mark elements that contain no textual content

```
<br />
```

The **footer** element contains address and summary information.

The **aside** element contains extra content on the page.

Exploring the History of the World Wide Web

Before you start creating a Web page for Dave, it will be helpful to first look at the history of the Web and the development of HTML. You'll start by reviewing networks and learn how they led to the creation of the World Wide Web.

Networks

A **network** is a structure that allows devices known as **nodes** or **hosts** to be linked together to share information and services. Hosts can include devices such as computers, printers, and scanners because they are all capable of sending and receiving data electronically over a network.

A host that provides information or a service is called a **server**. For example, a **print server** is a network host that provides printing services to the network; a **file server** is a host that provides storage space for saving and retrieving files. A computer or other device that receives a service is called a **client**. Networks can follow several different designs based on the relationship between the servers and the clients. One of the most commonly used designs is the **client-server network** in which several clients access information provided by one or more servers. You might be using such a network to access your data files for this tutorial.

Networks can also be classified based on the range they cover. A network confined to a small geographic area, such as within a building or department, is referred to as a **local area network** or **LAN**. A network that covers a wider area, such as several buildings or cities, is called a **wide area network** or **WAN**. Wide area networks typically consist of two or more interconnected local area networks.

The largest WAN in existence is the **Internet**, which incorporates an almost uncountable number of networks and hosts involving computers, mobile phones, PDAs, MP3 players, gaming systems, and television stations. Like many business owners, Dave uses the Internet to advertise his business to potential customers.

Locating Information on a Network

One of the biggest obstacles to effectively using the Internet is the network's sheer scope and size. Most of the early Internet tools required users to master a bewildering array of terms, acronyms, and commands. Because network users had to be well versed in computers and network technology, Internet use was limited to universities and the government. To make the Internet accessible to the general public, it needed to be easier to use. The solution turned out to be the World Wide Web.

The foundations for the **World Wide Web**, or the **Web** for short, were laid in 1989 by Timothy Berners-Lee and other researchers at the CERN nuclear research facility near Geneva, Switzerland. They needed an information system that would make it easy for their researchers to locate and share data on the CERN network with minimal training and support. To meet this need, they developed a system of hypertext documents that enabled users to easily navigate from one topic to another. **Hypertext** is a method of organization in which data sources are interconnected through a series of **links** or hyperlinks that users can activate to jump from one piece of information to another. Hypertext is ideally suited for the Internet because end users do not need to know where a particular document, information source, or service is located—they need to know only how to activate the link. The fact that the Internet and the World Wide Web are synonymous in many users' minds is a testament to the success of the hypertext approach.

Web Pages and Web Servers

Each document on the World Wide Web is referred to as a **Web page** and is stored on a **Web server**. When you access a Web page, a **Web browser** retrieves the page from its Web server and renders it on your computer or other device.

The earliest browsers, known as **text-based browsers**, were limited to displaying only text. Today's browsers are capable of handling text, images, audio, video, and interactive programs. In the early days of the Internet, Web browsing was limited to computers. Now browsers are installed on devices such as mobile phones, cars, handheld media devices, and gaming systems, to name only a few. How does a Web page work with so many combinations of browsers and devices? To understand, you need to look at how Web pages are created.

Introducing HTML

Web pages are text files written in **Hypertext Markup Language** (**HTML**). We've already discussed hypertext, but what is a markup language? A **markup language** is a language that describes the content and structure of a document by identifying, or **tagging**, different elements in the document. For example, this tutorial contains paragraphs, figure captions, page headings, and so forth; each of these items could be tagged as a distinct element using a markup language. Thus, HTML is a markup language that supports both hypertext and the tagging of distinct document elements.

The History of HTML

HTML evolved as the Web itself evolved. Thus, in order to fully appreciate the nuances of HTML, it's a good idea to review the language's history. The first popular markup language was the **Standard Generalized Markup Language** (**SGML**). Introduced in the 1980s, SGML is device- and system-independent, meaning that it can be applied to almost any type of document stored in almost any format. While powerful, SGML is also quite complex; for this reason, SGML is limited to those organizations that can afford the cost and overhead of maintaining complex SGML environments. However, SGML can also be used to create other markup languages that are tailored to specific tasks and are simpler to use and maintain. HTML is one of the languages created with SGML.

In the early years after HTML was created, no single organization was responsible for the language. Web developers were free to define and modify HTML in whatever ways they thought best. This led to incompatibilities between the various browsers and, as a result, Web page authors faced the challenge of writing HTML code that would satisfy different browsers and browser versions.

Ultimately, a group of Web designers and programmers called the **World Wide Web Consortium**, or the **W3C**, created a set of standards or specifications for all browser manufacturers to follow. The W3C has no enforcement power; but because using a uniform language is in everyone's best interest, the W3C's recommendations are usually followed, though not always immediately. For more information on the W3C and the services it offers, see its Web site at *www.w3.org*.

As HTML evolves, earlier features of the language are often **deprecated**, or phased out. While deprecated features might not be part of the current specification for HTML, that doesn't mean that you won't encounter them in your work—indeed, if you are maintaining older Web sites, you will often need to be able to interpret code from earlier versions of HTML.

XHTML and the Development of HTML5

Near the end of the 1990s, the W3C released the final specifications for the 4th version of HTML, called HTML 4, and began charting a course for the next version. The path chosen by the W3C was to reformulate HTML in terms of XML. **XML (Extensible Markup Language)** is a compact offshoot of SGML and is used to define new markup languages, known as **XML vocabularies**. A document based on an XML vocabulary is forced to obey specific rules for content and structure to avoid being rejected as invalid. By contrast, HTML allows for a wide variety in syntax between one HTML document and another. Another important aspect of XML is that several XML vocabularies can be combined within a single document, making it easier to extend XML into different areas of application.

The W3C developed an XML vocabulary that was a stricter version of HTML4, known as **XHTML (Extensible Hypertext Markup Language)**. XHTML was designed to confront some of the problems associated with the various competing versions of HTML and to better integrate HTML with other markup languages. Because XHTML was an XML version of HTML, most of what Web designers used with HTML could be applied to XHTML with only a few modifications, and many tools and features associated with XML could be easily applied to XHTML.

By 2002, the W3C had released the specifications for XHTML 1.1. This version was intended to be only a minor upgrade on the way to **XHTML 2.0**, which would contain a set of XML vocabularies moving HTML into the future with robust support for multimedia, social networking, interactive Web forms, and other features needed by Web designers. One problem was that XHTML 2.0 would not be backward compatible with earlier versions of HTML and thus older Web sites could not be easily integrated with the proposed new standard.

Web designers rebelled at this development. In 2004, Ian Hickson, who was working for Opera Software at the time, proposed a different path. Hickson's proposal would have allowed for the creation of new Web applications while still maintaining backward compatibility with HTML 4. He argued that HTML was whatever the browser market determined it to be, and that trying to enforce a new specification that did not accommodate the needs and limitations of the market was a fruitless exercise.

Hickson's proposal was rejected by the W3C and, in response, a new group of Web designers and browser manufacturers formed the **Web Hypertext Application Technology Working Group (WHATWG)** with the mission to develop a rival version to XHTML 2.0, called **HTML5**. For several years, it was unclear which specification would represent the future of the Web; but by 2006, work on XHTML 2.0 had completely stalled. The W3C issued a new charter for an HTML Working Group to develop HTML5 as the next HTML specification. Work on XHTML 2.0 was halted in 2009, leaving HTML5 as the de facto standard for the next generation of HTML.

Figure 1-1	Versions of HTML

Version	Date	Description
HTML1.0	1989	The first public version of HTML.
HTML 2.0	1995	Added interactive elements including Web forms.
HTML 3.0	1996	A proposed replacement for HTML 2.0 that was never widely adopted.
HTML 3.2	1997	Included additional support for Web tables and expanded the options for interactive form elements and a scripting language.
HTML 4.01	1999	Added support for style sheets to give Web designers greater control over page layout and appearance, and provided support for multimedia elements such as audio and video. Current browsers support almost all of HTML 4.01.
XHTML 1.0	2001	A reformulation of HTML 4.01 in the XML language in order to provide enforceable standards for HTML content and to allow HTML to interact with other XML languages.
XHTML 1.1	2002	A minor update to XHTML 1.0 that allows for modularity and simplifies writing extensions to the language.
XHTML 2.0	discontinued	The follow-up version to XHTML 1.1 designed to fix some of the problems inherent in HTML 4.01 syntax. Work on this version was discontinued in 2009 due to lack of browser support.
HTML 5.0	In development	An update to HTML 4.01 that provides support for a variety of new features including semantic page elements, column layout, form validation, offline storage, and enhanced multimedia.
XHTML 5.0	In development	A version of HTML 5.0 written under the XML language; unlike XHTML 2.0, XHTML 5.0 will be backward compatible with XHTML 1.1.

Figure 1-1 summarizes the various versions of HTML that have been developed over the past 20 years. You may be wondering how on Earth anything can be written with so many versions of HTML to consider. At the time of this writing, you can write your code following the standards of HTML 4.01 or XHTML 1.1 and be assured that it will be supported by all major browsers. Many features of HTML5 are also being rapidly adopted by the market even as work continues on developing the language. HTML5 is the future, but the challenges for Web designers today lie in knowing which parts of HTML5 are supported by which browsers, and in developing strategies for supporting older browsers even as HTML5 is being implemented.

In this book you'll use HTML5 code for those features that have already achieved support among current browsers, but you'll also learn the standards used for HTML 4.01 and XHTML 1.1 and practice writing code that will support both current and older browsers.

HTML and Style Sheets

HTML marks the different parts of a document, but it does not indicate how document content should be displayed by browsers. This is a necessary facet of HTML because a Web page author has no control over what device will actually view his or her document. An end user might be using a large-screen television monitor, a mobile phone, or even a device that renders Web pages in Braille or in aural speech.

For this reason, the exact appearance of each page element is described in a separate document known as a **style sheet**. Each browser has its own **internal style sheet** that specifies the appearance of different HTML elements. For example, content that is marked as containing the text of an address is rendered by most Web browsers in italic, while major headings usually appear in large bold-faced fonts.

A Web page author can also create a style sheet that takes precedence over the internal style sheets of browsers. In addition, an author can create multiple style sheets for different output devices: one for rendering a page on a computer screen, another for printed output, and another for rendering the page aurally. In each case, the markup of the document content is the same, but the presentation is determined by the style sheet.

Tools for Creating HTML Documents

Because HTML documents are simple text files, you can create them using nothing more than a basic text editor such as Windows Notepad. Other software programs that enable you to create documents in different formats, such as Microsoft Word or Adobe Acrobat, include tools to convert their documents into HTML for quick and easy publishing on the Web.

If you intend to create a large Web site incorporating dozens of Web pages, you should invest in specialized Web publishing software to manage all of the code and extended features of your site. Programs such as Adobe Dreamweaver and Microsoft Expression Web are among the leaders in this field.

Since this book is focused on the HTML language itself and not how to work with different software programs, you'll need nothing more than a text editor and a Web browser to complete the assignments that follow.

Entering Elements and Attributes

Now that you've had a chance to review a brief history of the Web and the role of HTML in its development, you are ready to write your first HTML document for the J-Prop Shop. You'll start by studying the rules for entering HTML code.

Introducing HTML Tags

An HTML document is composed of **elements** that represent distinct items in the Web page, such as a paragraph, the page heading, or even the entire body of the page itself. Each element is marked within the HTML file by one or more **tags**. If an element contains text or another element, it is marked using a **two-sided tag set** in which an **opening tag** and a **closing tag** enclose the element content. The syntax of a two-sided tag set is

```
<element>content</element>
```

where *element* is the name of the element and *content* is the content of the element. For example, the following code marks a paragraph using a two-sided tag set:

```
<p>Welcome to the J-Prop Shop.</p>
```

In this example, the <p> tag marks the beginning of the paragraph, the text *Welcome to the J-Prop Shop.* is the content of the paragraph element, and the </p> tag marks the end of the paragraph. Elements can also contain other elements. For example, in the code

```
<p>Welcome to <em>Dave's Devil Sticks</em>.</p>
```

the paragraph tags enclose both the text of the paragraph and the tag set <em> ... </em>, which is used to mark content that should be treated by the browser as emphasized text. Note that the <em> tag set must be completely enclosed, or **nested**, within the <p> tags. It's improper to have tags overlap as in the following code sample:

```
<p>Welcome to <em>Dave's Devil Sticks.</p></em>
```

In this example, the closing </em> tag is placed *after* the closing </p> tag, which is improper because one element must be completely contained within another.

An element that does not enclose content is an **empty element** and it is marked with a **one-sided tag** using the syntax

```
<element />
```

where `element` is the name of the element. For example, you can mark a line break using the `br` element, which has the following syntax:

```
<br />
```

Since empty elements don't contain content, they're often employed to send directives to browsers regarding how a page should be rendered. A browser encountering the `br` element would insert a line break, causing the text of the next element in the document to be placed on a new line.

Specifying an Element Attribute

In addition to content, elements also support **attributes** that specify the use, the behavior, and in some cases the appearance of an element. Attribute values don't appear in the rendered Web page; rather, they provide information to the browser about the properties of the element.

To add an attribute to an element, you insert the attribute within the element's opening tag. For a two-sided tag, the syntax is:

```
<element attribute1="value1" attribute2="value2" ...>
   content
</element>
```

Attributes are added to one-sided tags in the same way:

```
<element attribute1="value1" attribute2="value2" ... />
```

In these examples, `attribute1`, `attribute2`, etc. are the names of attributes associated with the element, and `value1`, `value2`, etc. are the values of those attributes. For instance, the following code adds the `id` attribute to a paragraph marked with the `p` element:

```
<p id="opening">Welcome to the J-Prop Shop.</p>
```

A browser interpreting this code would recognize that the text *Welcome to the J-Prop Shop.* should be treated as a paragraph and given the id value *opening*.

> **TIP**
>
> Attributes can be listed in any order, but they must be separated from one another by a blank space and enclosed within single or double quotation marks.

REFERENCE

Adding an Attribute to an Element

• To add an element attribute, use the format

```
<element attribute1="value1"
        attribute2="value2" ...>content</element>
```

where `attribute1`, `attribute2`, etc. are the names of attributes associated with the element, and `value1`, `value2`, etc. are the values of those attributes.

White Space and HTML

Since an HTML file is a text file, it's composed of text characters and white space. **White space** includes the blank spaces, tabs, and line breaks found within the file. As far as a browser is concerned, there is no difference between a blank space, a tab, or a line break. Browsers also ignore consecutive occurrences of white space, collapsing extra white space characters into a single blank space. Thus, browsers treat the following paragraph elements in the same way:

```
<p>Welcome to the J-Prop Shop.</p>


<p>
    Welcome to the J-Prop Shop.
</p>


<p>Welcome
to the J-Prop Shop.</p>


<p>Welcome   to    the    J-Prop    Shop.</p>
```

Because HTML handles white space in this way, you can make your code easier for others to read by indenting lines and adding extra blank lines to separate one tag from another in the file.

HTML5 and XHTML Syntax

The rules that govern how code should be entered are called **syntax**. The way that HTML has been implemented by most browsers through the Web's history has allowed for minor variations in syntax. One reason for the success of the Web is that HTML has made it easy for non-programmers to write and edit code without being ensnarled by syntax violations.

On the other hand, XHTML forces strict syntax on page authors. If an author's code does not follow the rules, browsers do not render the page. One advantage of this approach is that it forces authors to write clear and more concise code; indeed, one of the driving forces behind the development of XHTML was the desire to clean up some of the messy and inconsistent code found on the Web.

For example, XHTML requires that all tag names be placed in lowercase letters and that all attribute values be enclosed within quotation marks. HTML allows either uppercase or lowercase tag names and does not require attribute values to be quoted. In addition, XHTML requires that every one-sided tag be entered with a closing slash: for instance, the br element must be entered as `<br />` for XHTML compatibility. Most browsers, however, accept HTML code in which one-sided tags are entered without closing slashes; thus, the br element could be entered either as `<br>` or as `<br />`.

HTML5 supports the informal standards accepted by most browsers and will continue to allow for minor variations in syntax. However, it is still good practice to write all code to be XHTML compliant whenever possible, since it will allow that code to be easily transferred to XHTML environments if necessary.

Exploring the Structure of an HTML Document

The structure of an HTML document consists of different elements nested within each other in a hierarchy of elements. The top element in that hierarchy is the **html element**, which contains all of the other elements within an HTML file. Directly below the html element in the hierarchy are the head and body elements. The **head element** contains general information about the document—for example, the document's title, or a list of keywords that would aid search engines in directing interested users to the page. The **body element** contains all of the content that appears in the rendered Web page. Thus, the general structure of an HTML file is

```
<html>
    <head>
        head content
    </head>
    <body>
        body content
    </body>
</html>
```

where *head content* and *body content* are the content you want to place within the document's head and body. Note that the body element is always placed after the head element.

The Document Type Declaration

Prior to the opening `<html>` tag, many HTML files also include a **Document Type Declaration**, or **doctype**, to indicate the type of markup language used in the document. The doctype is used by **validators**, which are programs that examine document code to ensure that it meets all the syntax requirements of the specified language. All XHTML files require a doctype because those documents must be validated against a set of standards.

Most current browsers also use the presence or absence of a doctype to decide which mode they should use to render a document in a process known as **doctype switching**. If a doctype is included, such browsers render the Web page in **standards mode**, in accordance with the most current specifications of the language. If no doctype is provided, these browsers render the document in **quirks mode** based on practices followed in the 1990s. The differences can be striking. Figure 1-2 shows an example of two documents rendered by Internet Explorer under standards mode and quirks mode. The only difference in the code between these two documents is the presence or absence of a doctype, but the browser renders the two documents very differently.

Figure 1-2	A Web page rendered in standards mode and quirks mode

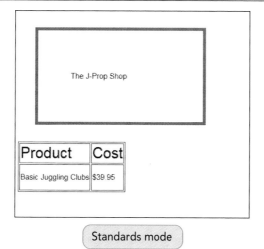

Standards mode

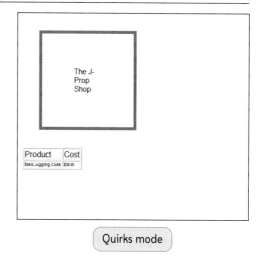

Quirks mode

Different HTML versions have different doctypes. The doctype for HTML 4.01 is:

```
<!DOCTYPE HTML PUBLIC "-//W3C//DTD HTML 4.01/EN"
    "http://www.w3.org/TR/html4/strict.dtd">
```

The doctype for XHTML is:

```
<!DOCTYPE html PUBLIC "-//W3C//DTD XHTML 1.0 Strict//EN"
    "http://www.w3.org/TR/xhtml1/DTD/xhtml1-strict.dtd">
```

Finally, the doctype for HTML5 is much simpler than what was required for HTML 4.01 or XHTML:

```
<!DOCTYPE html>
```

TIP

Unless you are working with a legacy page that absolutely needs to be compatible with old browsers from the 1990s, you should always include a doctype and put your browser in standards mode.

HTML5 documents should always be opened in standards mode because they are based on the latest specifications for the HTML language.

You can learn more about standards mode and quirks mode by searching the Web for examples of the differences between the two modes.

Creating the Initial Document

Now that you've seen the basic structure of an HTML document, you are ready to begin creating the sample Web page for Dave's Web site.

REFERENCE

Creating the Basic Structure of an HTML Document

Enter the HTML tags

```
doctype
<html>
    <head>
        head content
    </head>
    <body>
        body content
    </body>
</html>
```

where *doctype* is the Document Type Declaration, and *head content* and *body content* are the content of the document's head and body.

You can start creating Dave's Web page using a basic editor such as Windows Notepad. Since Dave wants his document to be based on HTML5, you'll use the HTML5 doctype in your file.

To create the basic structure of an HTML document:

1. Start your text editor, opening a blank text document.

   Trouble? If you don't know how to start or use your text editor, ask your instructor or technical support person for help. Note that some editors do not save files in text file format by default, so check your editor's documentation to ensure that you are creating a basic text document.

Make sure you include the exclamation point (!) within the doctype; otherwise, browsers will not recognize the doctype.

2. Type the following lines of code in your document. Press the **Enter** key after each line. Press the **Enter** key twice for a blank line between lines of code. See Figure 1-3.

```
<!DOCTYPE html>
<html>

    <head>
    </head>

    <body>
    </body>

</html>
```

| Figure 1-3 | Basic structure of an HTML file |

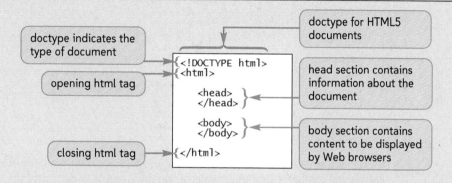

3. Save the file as **jprop.htm** in the tutorial.01\tutorial folder included with your Data Files.

Trouble? If you are using the Windows Notepad text editor to create your HTML file, make sure you don't save the file with the extension *.txt*, which is the default file extension for Notepad. Instead, save the file with the file extension *.htm* or *.html*. Using the incorrect file extension might make the file unreadable to Web browsers, which require file extensions of *.htm* or *.html*.

TIP

To make it easier to link to your Web pages, follow the Internet convention of naming HTML files and folders using only lowercase letters with no spaces.

Now that you've entered the basic structure of your HTML file, you can start entering the content of the head element.

Marking the Head Element

In general, the head element is where you provide browsers with information about your document. This can include the page's title, the location of any style sheets used with the document, the location of any programs that browsers should run when they load the page, and information for use by search engines to aid users in locating the Web site.

Defining the Page Title

The first element you'll add to the head of Dave's document is the title element, which has the syntax

```
<title>document title</title>
```

where *document title* is the text of the document title. The document title is not displayed within the page, but is usually displayed in a browser's title bar or on a browser tab. The document title is also used by search engines like Google or Yahoo! when compiling an index of search results.

To add a title to your Web page:

1. Click at the end of the opening `<head>` tag, and then press the **Enter** key to insert a new line in your text editor.

2. Press the **Spacebar** several times to indent the new line of code, and then type `<title>The J-Prop Shop</title>` as shown in Figure 1-4.

Figure 1-4 **Specifying the page title**

```
<!DOCTYPE html>
<html>

   <head>
      <title>The J-Prop Shop</title>
   </head>

   <body>
   </body>

</html>
```

> text will appear in browser title bar or on browser tab

Adding Comments

As you write your HTML file, you can add notes or comments about your code. These comments might include the name of the document's author and the date the document was created. Such notes are not intended to be displayed by browsers, but are instead used to help explain your code to yourself and others. To add notes or comments, insert a **comment tag** using the syntax

```
<!-- comment -->
```

where `comment` is the text of the comment or note. For example, the following code inserts a comment describing the page you'll create for Dave's business:

```
<!-- Sample page for the J-Prop Shop -->
```

A comment can also be spread out over several lines as follows:

```
<!-- Sample page for the J-Prop Shop.
     Created by Dave Vinet -->
```

Because they are ignored by the browser, comments can be added anywhere within the `html` element.

REFERENCE

Adding an HTML Comment

To insert an HTML comment anywhere within your document, enter

```
<!-- comment -->
```

where `comment` is the text of the HTML comment.

You'll add a comment to the *jprop.htm* file, identifying the author and purpose of this document.

To add a comment to the document head:

1. Click at the end of the opening `<head>` tag, and then press the **Enter** key to insert a new line in your text editor directly above the opening `<title>` tag.

2. Type the following lines of code as shown in Figure 1-5:

```
<!-- The J-Prop Shop Sample Page
     Author: your name
     Date:   the date
-->
```

where *your name* is your name and *the date* is the current date.

Figure 1-5   Adding comments to the HTML file

```
<!DOCTYPE html>
<html>

   <head>
      <!-- The J-Prop Shop Sample Page
           Author: David Vinet
           Date:   3/1/2014
      -->
      <title>The J-Prop Shop</title>
   </head>

   <body>
   </body>

</html>
```

multi-line comment describing the document

Displaying an HTML File

As you continue modifying the HTML code, you should occasionally view the page with your Web browser to verify that you have not introduced any errors. You might even want to view the results using different browsers to check for compatibility. In this book, Web pages are displayed using the Windows Internet Explorer 9 browser. Be aware that if you are using a different browser or a different operating system, you might see slight differences in the layout and appearance of the page.

To view Dave's Web page:

1. Save your changes to the **jprop.htm** file.

2. Start your Web browser. You do not need to be connected to the Internet to view local files stored on your computer.

   Trouble? If you start your browser and are not connected to the Internet, you might get a warning message. Click the OK button to ignore the message and continue.

3. After your browser loads its home page, open the **jprop.htm** file from the tutorial.01\tutorial folder.

   Trouble? If you're not sure how to open a local file with your browser, check for an Open or Open File command under the browser's File menu. If you are still having problems accessing the *jprop.htm* file, talk to your instructor or technical resource person.

Your browser displays the Web page shown in Figure 1-6. Note that in this case, the page title appears in the browser tab; in other cases, it will appear in the browser's title bar. The page itself is empty because you have not yet added any content to the body element.

| Figure 1-6 | Viewing the initial HTML file in a Web browser |

document title appears in the browser tab

no content appears in the page body

Converting an HTML Document into XHTML

INSIGHT

There is considerable overlap between HTML and XHTML. You can quickly change an HTML document into an XHTML document just by altering the first three lines of code. To convert an HTML file into an XHTML file, replace the doctype and the opening `<html>` tag with the following:

```
<?xml version="1.0" encoding="UTF-8" standalone="no" ?>
<!DOCTYPE html PUBLIC "-//W3C//DTD XHTML 1.0 Strict//EN"
   "http://www.w3.org/TR/xhtml1/DTD/xhtml1-strict.dtd">
<html xmlns="http://www.w3.org/1999/xhtml">
```

Since XHTML is an XML vocabulary, the first line notifies browsers that the document is an XML file. The version number—1.0—tells the browser that the file is written in XML 1.0. The second line provides the doctype for an XHTML document written under a strict interpretation of XHTML syntax. The third line of the file contains the opening `<html>` tag. In XHTML, the `<html>` tag must include what is known as a **namespace declaration** indicating that any markup tags in the document should, by default, be considered part of the XHTML language. Because XML documents can contain a mixture of several different vocabularies, the namespace declaration is necessary to specify the default language of the document. With these three lines in place, browsers will recognize the file as an XHTML document.

Defining the Structure of the Page Body

Now that you've marked the document head and inserted a page title, you'll turn to the contents of the body of the Web page. It's always a good idea to plan your Web page before you start coding it. You can do this by drawing a sketch or by creating a sample document within a word processor. Your preparatory work can weed out textual errors or point to potential problems in your page layout. In this case, Dave has already drawn up a flyer that he's passed out at juggling and circus conventions. Figure 1-7 shows the handout, which provides information about Dave's company and his products.

Figure 1-7   Dave's flyer

Quality Juggling and Circus Props

Welcome

If you're looking for high-quality, hand-crafted juggling and circus products, the J-Prop Shop is the store for you. I've designed and built props for the past 35 years, and my products have been used by professional entertainers and hobbyists throughout the world. Our prices are reasonable and our quality is excellent.

Specials This Month

The following devil sticks are available at a special discount for the entire month of May:

- **Basic Stick ($19.95)** The easiest stick to learn with, but "grippy" enough for the most demanding tricks. Comes in red, green, and blue.
- **Flower Stick ($24.95)** A graceful stick with colored tassels. Flower Sticks float slowly, making them ideal for beginners.
- **Master Stick ($39.95)** Our most popular stick is shorter and heavier for fast play and more advanced tricks. Each Master Stick is available in custom colors.
- **Glow Stick ($29.95)** The Glow Stick shines brightly at night (without the danger of a fire stick).

Quality Tested

Every item I create is checked and tested before being shipped out to assure perfect quality. I take pride in every one of my juggling props and I want my customers to feel that same pride.

Customer Comments

Here are a few select quotes from our happy family of customers and associates:

"I'm more than happy to recommend Dave Vinet's products. I came upon his work 10 years ago and was immediately impressed by his craftsmanship. He provides well-balanced and attractive props which are the perfect complement to my performances."
— Thomas Gage, Circus England

"Dave Vinet makes the best juggling equipment on the planet. Period."
— Douglas Pederson, Street-Wise Shows

"David has been my main supplier for 20 years. I have never had a problem with his equipment and his service is impeccable."
— Linda Unger, Linda & Louis

THE J-PROP SHOP • 541 WEST HIGHLAND DRIVE • AUBURN, ME 04210 • (207) 555 - 9001

Dave's flyer contains several elements that are common to many Web pages, as shown in Figure 1-8. A header displays the company's logo and a footer displays contact information for the J-Prop Shop. The main section, which describes Dave's business, includes several subsections, also known as articles. A second section that appears as a sidebar displays quotes from some J-Prop customers.

Figure 1-8	Structure of Dave's Web page

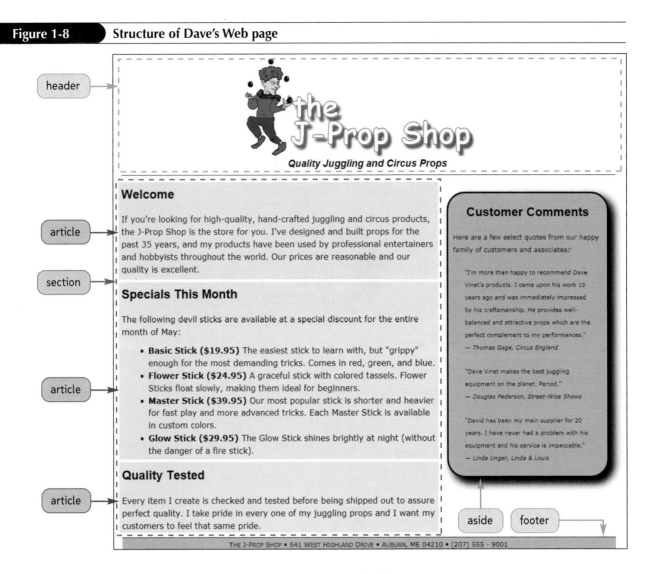

Working with HTML5 Structural Elements

Each of these parts of Dave's document can be marked using HTML5 **structural elements**, which are the elements that define the major sections of a Web page. Figure 1-9 describes some of these elements.

Figure 1-9	HTML5 structural elements

Structural Element	Description
article	A subsection covering a single topic
aside	Content containing tangential or side issues to the main topic of the page
footer	Content placed at the bottom of the page
header	Content placed at the top of the page
nav	A navigation list of hypertext links
section	A major topical area in the page

For example, to mark the header of your Web page, you would enter a `header` element within the page body, using the syntax

```
<header>
    header content
</header>
```

where *header content* is the page content that you want displayed within the page header. One of the reasons we want to define these structural elements is that we can write styles for them and define the layout of the Web page content.

REFERENCE

Marking Structural Elements in HTML5

- To mark the page header, use the `header` element.
- To mark the page footer, use the `footer` element.
- To mark a main section of page content, use the `section` element.
- To mark a sidebar, use the `aside` element.
- To mark an article, use the `article` element.

Based on Dave's sample document shown in Figure 1-8, you'll add the `header`, `section`, `aside`, and `footer` structural elements to your HTML file.

To insert the HTML5 structural elements:

1. Return to the **jprop.htm** file in your text editor.

2. Within the `body` element, insert the following tags as shown in Figure 1-10:

```
<header>
</header>

<section>
</section>

<aside>
</aside>

<footer>
</footer>
```

Figure 1-10   **Inserting structural elements**

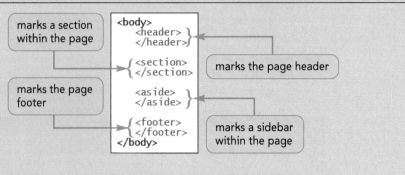

3. Save your changes to the file.

Structural elements can also be nested within one another. In the structure of Dave's page from Figure 1-8, notice that the section element contains three article elements. Add this content to your HTML file by nesting three `article` elements within the `section` element.

To add three article elements:

1. Within the `section` element, insert the following code as shown in Figure 1-11:

```
<article>
</article>

<article>
</article>

<article>
</article>
```

Figure 1-11   **Inserting nested elements**

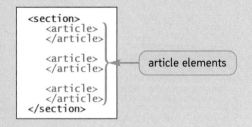

2. Save your changes to the file.

Marking a Section with the `div` Element

The structural elements are part of the current specifications for HTML5, but they are not part of HTML 4.01 or XHTML. Pages written to those languages instead use the **div element** to identify different page divisions. The syntax of the `div` element is

```
<div id="id">
    content
</div>
```

where *id* is a unique name assigned to the division and *content* is page content contained within the division. While not required, the `id` attribute is useful to distinguish one `div` element from another. This becomes particularly important if you apply different styles to different page divisions.

Figure 1-12 shows how the same page layout marked up using structural elements under HTML5 would be marked up in HTML 4.01 using the `div` element.

Figure 1-12	**Structural elements in HTML5 and HTML 4.01**

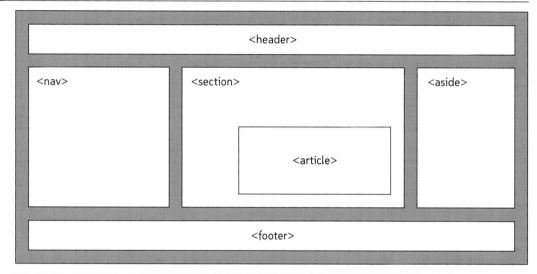

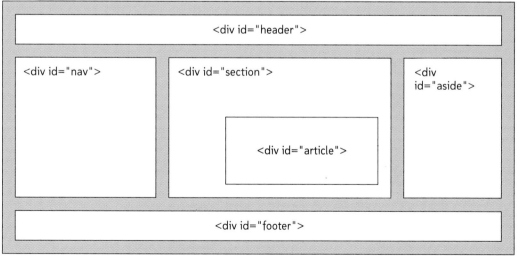

You can use either HTML5's structural elements or HTML 4.01's `div` elements to identify the major sections of your document. The HTML5 approach is preferred because it represents the future standard of the Web, and structural elements are more descriptive than the generic `div` element. One problem with the `div` element is that there are no rules for id names. One Web designer might identify the page heading with the id name *header* while another designer might use *heading* or *top*. This makes it harder for Web search engines to identify the main topics of interest in each Web page.

PROSKILLS

Written Communication: Writing Effective HTML Code

Part of writing good HTML code is being aware of the requirements of various browsers and devices, as well as understanding the different versions of the language. Here are a few guidelines for writing good HTML code:

- *Become well versed in the history of HTML and the various versions of HTML and XHTML.* Unlike other languages, HTML's history does impact how you write your code.
- *Know your market.* Do you have to support older browsers, or have your clients standardized on one particular browser or browser version? Will your Web pages be viewed on a single device such as a computer, or do you have to support a variety of devices?
- *Test your code on several different browsers and browser versions.* Don't assume that if your page works in one browser it will work in other browsers, or even in earlier versions of the same browser. Also check on the speed of the connection. A large file that performs well with a high-speed connection might be unusable with a dial-up connection.
- *Read the documentation on the different versions of HTML and XHTML at the W3C Web site and keep up to date with the latest developments in the language.*

In general, any HTML code that you write should be compatible with the current versions of the following browsers: Internet Explorer (Windows), Firefox (Windows and Macintosh), Safari (Windows and Macintosh), Chrome (Windows and Macintosh), and Opera (Windows and Macintosh). In addition, you should also view your pages on a variety of devices including laptops, mobile phones, and tablets. To effectively communicate with customers and users, you need to make sure your Web site is always readable.

At this point, you've created the basic framework of Dave's Web page. In the next session, you'll insert the page content and learn how to apply a visual style to that content to create a nicely formatted Web page. If you want to take a break before starting the next session, you can close any open files or applications.

REVIEW

Session 1.1 Quick Check

1. What is a markup language?
2. What is XHTML? How does XHTML differ from HTML?
3. What is the W3C? What is the WHATWG?
4. What is a doctype? What are two uses of the doctype?
5. What is incorrect about the syntax of the following code?

   ```
   <p>Welcome to the <em>J-Prop Shop</p></em>
   ```

6. What is white space? How does HTML treat consecutive occurrences of white space?
7. What structural element would you use to mark a sidebar?
8. What structural element would you use to mark the page footer?

SESSION 1.2 VISUAL OVERVIEW

The **h2** element marks a heading.

The **p** element marks a paragraph.

The **ul** element marks an unordered list.

The **li** element marks an item in the list.

The **strong** element is a text-level element that marks strong or bold text.

HTML code

```
<h2>Welcome</h2>
<p>If you're looking for high-qu
   juggling and circus products,
   the store for you. I've desig
   for the past 35 years, and my
   used by professional entertai
   throughout the world. Our pri
   our quality is excellent.
</p>
```

```
<ul>
   <li><strong>Basic Stick ($19
      The easiest stick to lea
      for the most demanding t
      and blue.
   </li>
   <li><strong>Flower Stick ($2
      A graceful stick with co
      float slowly, making the
   </li>
   <li><strong>Master Stick ($3
      Our most popular stick i
      fast play and more advan
      is available in custom c
   </li>
   <li><strong>Glow Stick ($29.
      The Glow Stick shines br
      the danger of a fire sti
   </li>
</ul>
```

Resulting Web page

Quality Juggling and Circus Props

Welcome

If you're looking for high-quality, hand-crafted juggling and circus products, the J-Prop Shop is the store for you. I've designed and built props for the past 35 years, and my products have been used by professional entertainers and hobbyists throughout the world. Our prices are reasonable and our quality is excellent.

Specials This Month

The following devil sticks are available at a special discount for the entire month of May:

- **Basic Stick ($19.95)** The easiest stick to learn with, but "grippy" enough for the most demanding tricks. Comes in red, green, and blue.
- **Flower Stick ($24.95)** A graceful stick with colored tassels. Flower Sticks float slowly, making them ideal for beginners.
- **Master Stick ($39.95)** Our most popular stick is shorter and heavier for fast play and more advanced tricks. Each Master Stick is available in custom colors.
- **Glow Stick ($29.95)** The Glow Stick shines brightly at night (without the danger of a fire stick).

Quality Tested

Every item I create is checked and tested before being shipped out to assure perfect quality. I take pride in every one of my juggling props and I want my customers to feel that same pride.

THE J-PROP SHOP • 541 WEST HIGHLAND DRIVE • AUBURN, ME 04210 • (207) 555

The **address** element marks an address or contact info.

```
<address>The J-Prop Shop &bull;
   541 West Highland Drive &bull;
   Auburn, ME 04210 &bull;
   (207) 555 - 9001
</address>
```

The **•** entity represents the bullet character.

PAGE CONTENT ELEMENTS

HTML code

The **hgroup** element groups main headings and subheadings.

The **img** element is used to insert images into the Web page.

```
<hgroup>
    <h1>
        <img src="jpslogo.png" alt="The J-Prop Shop" />
    </h1>
    <h2>
        Quality Juggling and Circus Props
    </h2>
</hgroup>
```

```
<blockquote>
    <p>"I'm more than happy to reco
        products. I came upon his wo
        was immediately impressed by
        He provides well-balanced an
        props which are the perfect
        performances."
    <br />
    &#8212; <cite>Thomas Gage, C
    </p>
```

The **blockquote** element marks large blocks of quoted material.

The **cite** element marks a citation.

The **—** entity represents the em-dash character.

Customer Comments

Here are a few select quotes from our happy family of customers and associates:

"I'm more than happy to recommend Dave Vinet's products. I came upon his work 10 years ago and was immediately impressed by his craftsmanship. He provides well-balanced and attractive props which are the perfect complement to my performances."
— *Thomas Gage, Circus England*

"Dave Vinet makes the best juggling equipment on the planet. Period."
— *Douglas Pederson, Street-Wise Shows*

"David has been my main supplier for 20 years. I have never had a problem with his equipment and his service is impeccable."
— *Linda Unger, Linda & Louis*

A page rendered with the default browser style sheet

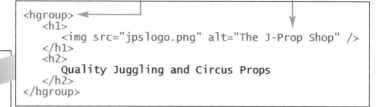

The same page rendered with a user-defined style sheet

```
<link href="jpsstyles.css" rel="stylesheet" type="text/css" />
```

The **link** element connects the Web page to the style sheet.

The href attribute indicates the name of the style sheet file.

The type attribute indicates the language of the style sheet.

Working with Grouping Elements

You're now ready to begin entering content into the body of Dave's Web page. The first elements you'll add are **grouping elements**, which are elements that contain content that is viewed as a distinct block within the Web page. Paragraphs, which were presented in the last session, are one example of a grouping element, as are page divisions marked using the div element. Figure 1-13 lists some of the commonly used grouping elements.

Figure 1-13	Grouping elements

Grouping Element	Description
address	Contact information (usually rendered as *italicized* text)
blockquote	An extended quotation (usually indented from the left and right margins)
dd	A definition from a description list
div	A generic grouping element
dl	A description list
dt	A definition term from a description list
figure	A figure or illustration (HTML5 only)
figcaption	The caption of a figure, which must be nested within the figure element (HTML5 only)
h*n*	A heading, where *n* is a value from 1 to 6, with h1 as the most prominent heading and h6 the least prominent (usually displayed in **bold** text)
li	A list item from an ordered or unordered list
ol	An ordered list
p	A paragraph
pre	Preformatted text, retaining all white space and special characters (usually displayed in a `fixed width` font)
ul	An unordered list

To explore how grouping elements are typically rendered by your Web browser, a demo page has been prepared for you.

To open the HTML Tags demo page:

1. Use your browser to open the **demo_html.htm** file from the tutorial.01\demo folder.

2. If your browser prompts you to allow code from the Web page to be run, click the **Allow blocked content** button.

Marking Content Headings

The first grouping elements you'll explore are **heading elements**, which contain the text of main headings on a Web page. They're often used for introducing new topics or for dividing the page into topical sections. The syntax to mark a heading element is

```
<hn>content</hn>
```

where *n* is an integer from 1 to 6. Content marked with <h1> tags is considered a major heading, and is usually displayed in large bold text. Content marked with <h2> through <h6> tags is used for subheadings, and is usually displayed in progressively smaller bold text.

Marking Grouping Content

- To mark a heading, enter
  `<hn>`*content*`</hn>`
  where *n* is an integer from 1 to 6 and *content* is the text of the heading.
- To mark a paragraph, enter
  `<p>`*content*`</p>`
- To mark a block quote, enter
  `<blockquote>`*content*`</blockquote>`

To see how these headings appear on your computer, use the demo page.

To view heading elements:

1. Click in the blue box in the lower-left corner of the demo page, type `<h1>The J-Prop Shop</h1>` and then press the **Enter** key to go to a new line.

2. Type `<h2>Quality Juggling and Circus Props</h2>`.

3. Click the **Preview Code** button located below the blue code window. Your browser displays a preview of how this code would appear in your Web browser (see Figure 1-14).

Figure 1-14	Previewing h1 and h2 headings

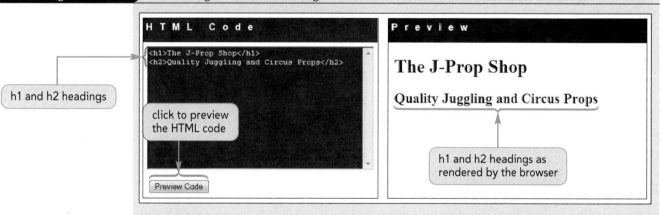

Trouble? If you are using a browser other than Internet Explorer 9 running on Windows 7, your screen might look slightly different from that shown in Figure 1-14.

4. To see how an h3 heading would look, change the opening tag for the store description from `<h2>` to `<h3>` and change the closing tag from `</h2>` to `</h3>`. Click the **Preview Code** button again.

Your browser renders the code again, this time with the store information displayed in a smaller font. If you continued to change the heading element from h3 to each of the elements down to h6, you would see the second line in the Preview box get progressively smaller.

It's important not to treat markup tags as simply a way of formatting the Web page. The h1 through h6 elements are used to identify headings, but the exact appearance of these headings depends on the browser and the device being used. While most browsers display an h1 heading in a larger font than an h2 heading, remember that the headings might not even be displayed at all. A screen reader, for example, doesn't display text, but rather conveys the presence of an h1 heading with increased volume or with special emphasis preceded by an extended pause.

Now that you've seen how to mark page headings, you can add them to Dave's Web page. The first heading Dave wants to add is an h1 heading containing the company's name. He also wants you to insert h2 headings in several places—as titles for the three articles on the page, as a title for the sidebar containing the customer comments, and as a subheading to the main heading on the page.

To add headings to Dave's document:

1. Return to the **jprop.htm** file in your text editor.

   Trouble? If you are using the Macintosh TextEdit program, you must select the *Ignore rich text commands* check box when reopening the file.

2. Within the header element, insert the following tags:

   ```
   <h1>The J-Prop Shop</h1>
   <h2>Quality Juggling and Circus Props</h2>
   ```

3. Within the first article element, insert the following h2 heading:

   ```
   <h2>Welcome</h2>
   ```

4. Within the second article element, insert

   ```
   <h2>Specials This Month</h2>
   ```

5. Within the third and final article element, insert

   ```
   <h2>Quality Tested</h2>
   ```

6. Finally, within the aside element, insert

   ```
   <h2>Customer Comments</h2>
   ```

   Figure 1-15 highlights the revised code in the file.

Figure 1-15   Inserting h1 and h2 headings

```
<body>
    <header>
        <h1>The J-Prop Shop</h1>
        <h2>Quality Juggling and Circus Props</h2>
    </header>

    <section>
        <article>
            <h2>Welcome</h2>
        </article>

        <article>
            <h2>Specials This Month</h2>
        </article>

        <article>
            <h2>Quality Tested</h2>
        </article>
    </section>

    <aside>
        <h2>Customer Comments</h2>
    </aside>

    <footer>
    </footer>
</body>
```

> **7.** Save your changes to the file and then reload or refresh the **jprop.htm** file in your Web browser. Figure 1-16 shows the initial view of the page body content.

Figure 1-16   Viewing h1 and h2 headings in Dave's document

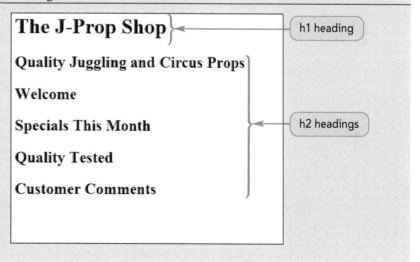

Grouping Headings

The interpretation of a particular heading depends on how it's used. For example, the h2 headings you just entered were used either to provide a title for articles or sections in the Web page or as a subtitle to the main title of the page. You can indicate that an h2 heading acts as a subtitle by grouping it with a main title heading using the **hgroup element**. The hgroup element uses the syntax

```
<hgroup>
    heading elements
</hgroup>
```

TIP

The hgroup element can contain only h1 through h6 elements or other hgroup elements.

where *heading elements* are elements marked with the <h1> through <h6> heading tags. The hgroup element was introduced in HTML5 and is not part of older HTML or XHTML specifications.

Group the first two headings in Dave's document to indicate that they should be interpreted as a main title and a subtitle.

To group the first two headings in the document:

1. Return to the **jprop.htm** file in your text editor.

2. Indent the first two headings in the document and then enclose them within <hgroup> tags as shown in Figure 1-17.

Figure 1-17   Grouping the h1 and h2 headings

h1 and h2 headings are grouped together

```
<body>
   <header>
      <hgroup>
         <h1>The J-Prop Shop</h1>
         <h2>Quality Juggling and Circus Props</h2>
      </hgroup>
   </header>
```

3. Save your changes to the file.

Marking Paragraph Elements

As you saw earlier, you can mark a paragraph element using the <p> tag, which has the syntax

```
<p>content</p>
```

where *content* is the content of the paragraph. In older HTML code, you might occasionally see paragraphs marked with only the opening <p> tags, omitting closing tags. In those situations, a <p> tag marks the start of each new paragraph. While this convention is still accepted by many browsers, it violates HTML's syntax rules. In addition, if you want XHTML-compliant code, you must always include closing tags.

Many articles on the J-Prop Shop page are enclosed within paragraphs. You'll add these paragraphs now.

To add four paragraphs to Dave's Web page:

1. Return to the **jprop.htm** file in your text editor.

2. Directly below the h2 heading *Welcome*, insert the following paragraph code, indented as shown in Figure 1-18:

```
<p>If you're looking for high-quality, hand-crafted
   juggling and circus products, the J-Prop Shop is
   the store for you. I've designed and built props
   for the past 35 years, and my products have been
   used by professional entertainers and hobbyists
   throughout the world. Our prices are reasonable and
   our quality is excellent.
</p>
```

3. Directly below the h2 heading *Specials This Month*, insert the following:

```
<p>The following devil sticks are available at a
   special discount for the entire month of May:
</p>
```

4. Directly below the h2 heading *Quality Tested*, insert the following:

```
<p>Every item I create is checked and tested before
   being shipped out to assure perfect quality. I take
   pride in every one of my juggling props and I want
   my customers to feel that same pride.
</p>
```

5. Finally, below the h2 heading *Customer Comments*, insert the following:

```
<p>Here are a few select quotes from our happy family
   of customers and associates:
</p>
```

Figure 1-18 highlights the newly added paragraphs in the document.

Figure 1-18   Adding paragraph elements

```
<section>
   <article>
      <h2>Welcome</h2>
      <p>If you're looking for high-quality, hand-crafted
         juggling and circus products, the J-Prop Shop is
         the store for you. I've designed and built props
         for the past 35 years, and my products have been
         used by professional entertainers and hobbyists
         throughout the world. Our prices are reasonable and
         our quality is excellent.
      </p>
   </article>

   <article>
      <h2>Specials This Month</h2>
      <p>The following devil sticks are available at a
         special discount for the entire month of May:
      </p>
   </article>

   <article>
      <h2>Quality Tested</h2>
      <p>Every item I create is checked and tested before
         being shipped out to assure perfect quality. I take
         pride in every one of my juggling props and I want
         my customers to feel that same pride.
      </p>
   </article>
</section>

<aside>
   <h2>Customer Comments</h2>
   <p>Here are a few select quotes from our happy family
      of customers and associates:
   </p>
</aside>
```

Trouble? Don't worry if your lines do not wrap at the same locations shown in Figure 1-18. Where the line wraps in the HTML code does not affect how the page is rendered by the browser.

6. Save your changes to the file and then refresh the **jprop.htm** file in your Web browser. Figure 1-19 shows the new paragraphs added to the Web page.

Figure 1-19 **Paragraphs in the Web page**

The J-Prop Shop

Quality Juggling and Circus Props

Welcome

If you're looking for high-quality, hand-crafted juggling and circus products, the J-Prop Shop is the store for you. I've designed and built props for the past 35 years, and my products have been used by professional entertainers and hobbyists throughout the world. Our prices are reasonable and our quality is excellent.

Specials This Month

The following devil sticks are available at a special discount for the entire month of May:

paragraphs

Quality Tested

Every item I create is checked and tested before being shipped out to assure perfect quality. I take pride in every one of my juggling props and I want my customers to feel that same pride.

Customer Comments

Here are a few select quotes from our happy family of customers and associates:

Marking a Block Quote

Next, Dave wants you to enter a few select quotes from his satisfied customers. You mark extended quotes with the HTML `blockquote` element, which uses the syntax

```
<blockquote>content</blockquote>
```

where *content* is the text of the quote. Most browsers render block quotes by indenting them to make it easier for readers to separate quoted material from the author's own words.

You'll add the customer comments as block quotes.

To create the customer comment block quotes:

1. Return to the **jprop.htm** file in your text editor.

2. Scroll down to the `aside` element, and after the paragraph within that element, insert the following block quote, as shown in Figure 1-20:

```
<blockquote>
   <p>"I'm more than happy to recommend Dave Vinet's
      products. I came upon his work 10 years ago and
      was immediately impressed by his craftsmanship.
      He provides well-balanced and attractive
      props which are the perfect complement to my
      performances."
   </p>
   <p>"Dave Vinet makes the best juggling equipment on
      the planet. Period."
   </p>
   <p>"David has been my main supplier for 20 years. I
      have never had a problem with his equipment and
      his service is impeccable."
   </p>
</blockquote>
```

Figure 1-20	Adding a block quote

```
<aside>
    <h2>Customer Comments</h2>
    <p>Here are a few select quotes from our happy family
        of customers and associates:
    </p>
    <blockquote>
        <p>"I'm more than happy to recommend Dave Vinet's
            products. I came upon his work 10 years ago and
            was immediately impressed by his craftsmanship.
            He provides well-balanced and attractive
            props which are the perfect complement to my
            performances."
        </p>
        <p>"Dave Vinet makes the best juggling equipment on
            the planet. Period."
        </p>
        <p>"David has been my main supplier for 20 years. I
            have never had a problem with his equipment and
            his service is impeccable."
        </p>
    </blockquote>
</aside>
```

3. Save your changes to the file, and then reload **jprop.htm** in your Web browser. Figure 1-21 shows the revised page with the quoted material.

Figure 1-21	Block quote in the Web page

Customer Comments

Here are a few select quotes from our happy family of customers and associates:

> "I'm more than happy to recommend Dave Vinet's products. I came upon his work 10 years ago and was immediately impressed by his craftsmanship. He provides well-balanced and attractive props which are the perfect complement to my performances."
>
> "Dave Vinet makes the best juggling equipment on the planet. Period."
>
> "David has been my main supplier for 20 years. I have never had a problem with his equipment and his service is impeccable."

quoted paragraphs are indented in the page

Note that the customer quote also included three paragraph elements nested within the `blockquote` element. The indentation applied by the browser to the block quote was also applied to any content within that element, so those paragraphs were indented even though browsers do not indent paragraphs by default.

Marking an Address

Dave wants to display the company's address at the bottom of the body of his page. Contact information such as addresses can be marked using the `address` element, which uses the syntax

```
<address>content</address>
```

where *content* is the contact information. Most browsers render addresses in italic. You'll use the `address` element to display the address of the J-Prop Shop.

To add the J-Prop Shop address:

▶ **1.** Return to the **jprop.htm** file in your text editor.

▶ **2.** Scroll down to the bottom of the file, and then within the `footer` element insert the following code, as shown in Figure 1-22:

```
<address>The J-Prop Shop
         541 West Highland Drive
         Auburn, ME 04210
         (207) 555 - 9001
</address>
```

Figure 1-22	Adding an address

```
<footer>
    <address>The J-Prop Shop
             541 West Highland Drive
             Auburn, ME 04210
             (207) 555 - 9001
    </address>
</footer>
</body>
```

▶ **3.** Save your changes to the file, and then refresh **jprop.htm** in your Web browser. Figure 1-23 shows the revised page with the address text.

Figure 1-23	Address as rendered in the Web page

Customer Comments

Here are a few select quotes from our happy family of customers and associates:

"I'm more than happy to recommend Dave Vinet's products. I came upon his work 10 years ago and was immediately impressed by his craftsmanship. He provides well-balanced and attractive props which are the perfect complement to my performances."

"Dave Vinet makes the best juggling equipment on the planet. Period."

"David has been my main supplier for 20 years. I have never had a problem with his equipment and his service is impeccable."

The J-Prop Shop 541 West Highland Drive Auburn, ME 04210 (207) 555 - 9001

address text is displayed in italic by default

The address text appears in italic at the bottom of the page. Note that even though you entered the company name, street address, city, state, and phone number on multiple lines, in the browser they all appear to run together on a single line. Remember that the browser ignores the occurrence of line breaks, tabs, and other white space in your text document. Shortly, you'll learn how to make this text more readable by adding a character symbol to separate the different parts of the address. For now, you'll leave the address text as it is.

Marking a List

Dave wants to display a list of products on this sample page. This information is presented on his flyer as a bulleted list. He wants something similar on the Web site. HTML supports three kinds of lists: ordered, unordered, and description.

REFERENCE

Marking Lists

- To mark an ordered list, enter
```
<ol>
    <li>item1</li>
    <li>item2</li>
...
</ol>
```
where *item1*, *item2*, and so forth are the items in the list.
- To mark an unordered list, enter
```
<ul>
    <li>item1</li>
    <li>item2</li>
...
</ul>
```
- To mark a description list, enter
```
<dl>
    <dt>term1</dt>
    <dd>description1</dd>
    <dt>term2</dt>
    <dd>description2a</dd>
    <dd>description2b</dd>
...
</dl>
```
where *term1*, *term2*, etc. are the terms in the list and *description1*, *description2a*, *description2b*, etc. are descriptions associated with the preceding terms.

Ordered Lists

Ordered lists are used for items that follow some defined sequential order, such as lists ordered from smallest to greatest or from oldest to youngest. The beginning of an ordered list is marked by the `<ol>` (ordered list) tag. Each item within an ordered list is marked using the `<li>` (list item) tag. The structure of an ordered list is therefore

```
<ol>
    <li>item1</li>
    <li>item2</li>
...
</ol>
```

where *item1*, *item2*, and so forth are the items in the list. To explore creating an ordered list, you'll return to the HTML demo page.

To create an ordered list:

1. Return to the **demo_html.htm** file in your Web browser.
2. Delete the HTML code in the left box and replace it with the following:
```
<ol>
    <li>First Item</li>
    <li>Second Item</li>
    <li>Third Item</li>
</ol>
```

3. Click the **Preview Code** button. Figure 1-24 shows how the browser renders the ordered list contents.

Figure 1-24 **Viewing an ordered list**

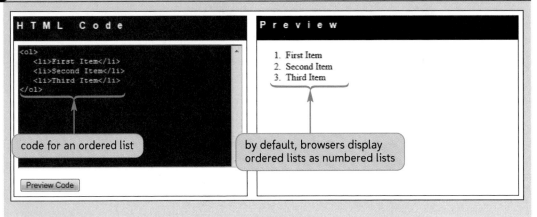

By default, entries in an ordered list are numbered, with the numbers added automatically by the browser.

Unordered Lists

To mark a list in which the items are not expected to occur in any specific order, you create an **unordered list**. The structure of ordered and unordered lists is the same, except that the list items for an unordered list are nested within the ul element, as follows:

```
<ul>
    <li>item1</li>
    <li>item2</li>
...
</ul>
```

You'll practice creating an unordered list with the demo page.

To create an unordered list:

1. Delete the HTML code in the left box and replace it with the following:

```
<ul>
    <li>Basic Stick</li>
    <li>Flower Stick</li>
    <li>Master Stick</li>
    <li>Glow Stick</li>
</ul>
```

2. Click the **Preview Code** button. Figure 1-25 shows how the browser renders the unordered list.

Figure 1-25   **Viewing an unordered list**

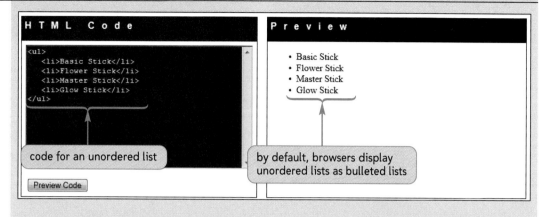

> **Trouble?** In some browsers, the list appears with diamond shapes rather than circular bullets.

By default, most browsers display unordered lists using a bullet symbol. The exact bullet symbol depends on the browser, but most browsers use a filled-in circle.

Nesting Lists

You can place one list inside of another to create several levels of list items. The top level of a nested list contains the major items, with each sublevel containing items of lesser importance. Most browsers differentiate the various levels by increasing the indentation and using a different list symbol at each level. You'll use the demo page to see how this works with unordered lists.

To create a nested list:

1. Click after the word *Stick* in the `<li>Basic Stick</li>` line, and then press the **Enter** key to insert a new blank line.

2. Indent the following code between the code `<li>Basic Stick` and the closing `</li>` tag:

```
<ul>
    <li>Red</li>
    <li>Blue</li>
    <li>Green</li>
</ul>
```

3. Click the **Preview Code** button. Figure 1-26 shows the resulting nested list in the browser.

Figure 1-26   Viewing a nested list

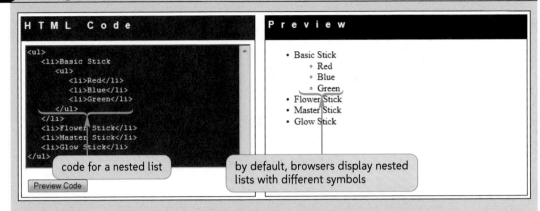

Trouble? Depending on your browser, the nested list of basic stick colors might appear with solid bullets rather than open circles.

The lower level of items is displayed using an open circle as the list bullet and additional indentation on the page. Once again, the exact format applied to these lists is determined by each browser's internal style sheet.

Description Lists

A third type of list is the **description list**, which contains a list of terms, each followed by its description. The structure of a description list is

```
<dl>
    <dt>term1</dt>
    <dd>description1</dd>
    <dt>term2</dt>
    <dd>description2a</dd>
    <dd>description2b</dd>
...
</dl>
```

where *term1, term2*, etc. are the terms in the list and *description1, description2a, description2b*, etc. are the descriptions associated with the terms. Note that description lists must follow a specified order, with each dt (definition term) element followed by one or more dd (definition description) elements.

You'll study how to work with description lists by returning to the demo page.

To create a description list:

1. Replace the code in the left box of the HTML demo page with

```
<dl>
    <dt>Basic Stick</dt>
    <dd>Easiest stick to learn</dd>
    <dt>Flower Stick</dt>
    <dd>A graceful stick with tassels</dd>
    <dt>Master Stick</dt>
    <dd>Our most popular stick</dd>
</dl>
```

2. Click the **Preview Code** button. Figure 1-27 shows the appearance of the description list in the browser.

Figure 1-27 **Viewing a description list**

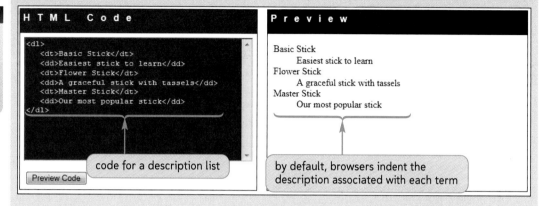

The demo page shows each term followed by its description, which is placed in a new block below the term and indented on the page. If you had included multiple dd elements for a single dt element, each description would have been contained within its own block and indented.

Now that you've experimented with the three types of HTML lists, you'll add an unordered list of products to Dave's Web page. By default, the product names will appear as a bulleted list.

To add an unordered list to Dave's Web page:

1. Return to the **jprop.htm** file in your text editor.

2. Within the Specials This Month article, directly below the p element, insert the following code, as shown in Figure 1-28:

```
<ul>
   <li>Basic Stick ($19.95)
      The easiest stick to learn with, but "grippy" enough
      for the most demanding tricks. Comes in red, green,
      and blue.
   </li>
   <li>Flower Stick ($24.95)
      A graceful stick with colored tassels. Flower Sticks
      float slowly, making them ideal for beginners.
   </li>
   <li>Master Stick ($39.95)
      Our most popular stick is shorter and heavier for
      fast play and more advanced tricks. Each Master Stick
      is available in custom colors.
   </li>
   <li>Glow Stick ($29.95)
      The Glow Stick shines brightly at night (without
      the danger of a fire stick).
   </li>
</ul>
```

Figure 1-28 Adding an unordered list

```
<article>
   <h2>Specials This Month</h2>
   <p>The following devil sticks are available at a
      special discount for the entire month of May:
   </p>
   <ul>
      <li>Basic Stick ($19.95)
         The easiest stick to learn with, but "grippy" enough
         for the most demanding tricks. Comes in red, green,
         and blue.
      </li>
      <li>Flower Stick ($24.95)
         A graceful stick with colored tassels. Flower Sticks
         float slowly, making them ideal for beginners.
      </li>
      <li>Master Stick ($39.95)
         Our most popular stick is shorter and heavier for
         fast play and more advanced tricks. Each Master Stick
         is available in custom colors.
      </li>
      <li>Glow Stick ($29.95)
         The Glow Stick shines brightly at night (without
         the danger of a fire stick).
      </li>
   </ul>

</article>
```

unordered list element

list item

3. Save your changes to the file, and then refresh the **jprop.htm** file in your Web browser. As shown in Figure 1-29, the list of products appears as a bulleted list in the middle of the page.

Figure 1-29 Unordered list as rendered in the Web page

Specials This Month

The following devil sticks are available at a special discount for the entire month of May:

unordered list items are displayed with bullet markers

- Basic Stick ($19.95) The easiest stick to learn with, but "grippy" enough for the most demanding tricks. Comes in red, green, and blue.
- Flower Stick ($24.95) A graceful stick with colored tassels. Flower Sticks float slowly, making them ideal for beginners.
- Master Stick ($39.95) Our most popular stick is shorter and heavier for fast play and more advanced tricks. Each Master Stick is available in custom colors.
- Glow Stick ($29.95) The Glow Stick shines brightly at night (without the danger of a fire stick).

Although you've added much of the text content to Dave's sample page, the page as rendered by the browser still looks nothing like the flyer shown in Figure 1-7. That's because all of the page elements have been rendered using your browser's internal style sheet. To change the page's appearance, you need to substitute your own style sheet for the browser's internal one.

Applying an External Style Sheet

Style sheets are written in the **Cascading Style Sheet (CSS)** language. Like HTML files, CSS files are text files and can be created and edited using a simple text editor. A style sheet file has the file extension *.css*, which distinguishes it from an HTML file. Dave already has a style sheet for his Web page stored in the file *jpsstyles.css*.

Linking to an External Style Sheet

To apply an external style sheet to a Web page, you create a link within the document head to the style sheet file using the `link` element

```
<link href="file" rel="stylesheet" type="text/css" />
```

where `file` is the filename and location of the style sheet file. When a browser loads the page, it substitutes the style from the external style sheet file for its own internal style sheet.

See how the format and layout of Dave's sample page change when the page is linked to the *jpsstyles.css* file.

To apply Dave's external style sheet:

1. Return to the **jprop.htm** file in your text editor.

2. Within the head element at the top of the file, insert the following link element, as shown in Figure 1-30:

```
<link href="jpsstyles.css" rel="stylesheet" type="text/css" />
```

Figure 1-30   Linking to the jpsstyles.css style sheet

```
<!DOCTYPE html>
<html>

    <head>
    <!-- The J-Prop Shop Sample Page
         Author: David Vinet
         Date:   3/1/2014
    -->
        <title>The J-Prop Shop</title>
        <link href="jpsstyles.css" rel="stylesheet" type="text/css" />
    </head>
```

link element

filename of style sheet

style sheet language

3. Save your changes to the file.

4. Reload the **jprop.htm** file in your Web browser. As shown in Figure 1-31, the format and the layout change to reflect the styles in Dave's style sheet.

Figure 1-31	**Web page rendered with the jpsstyles.css style sheet**

The J-Prop Shop
Quality Juggling and Circus Props

Welcome

If you're looking for high-quality, hand-crafted juggling and circus products, the J-Prop Shop is the store for you. I've designed and built props for the past 35 years, and my products have been used by professional entertainers and hobbyists throughout the world. Our prices are reasonable and our quality is excellent.

Specials This Month

The following devil sticks are available at a special discount for the entire month of May:

- Basic Stick ($19.95) The easiest stick to learn with, but "grippy" enough for the most demanding tricks. Comes in red, green, and blue.
- Flower Stick ($24.95) A graceful stick with colored tassels. Flower Sticks float slowly, making them ideal for beginners.
- Master Stick ($39.95) Our most popular stick is shorter and heavier for fast play and more advanced tricks. Each Master Stick is available in custom colors.
- Glow Stick ($29.95) The Glow Stick shines brightly at night (without the danger of a fire stick.)

Quality Tested

Every item I create is checked and tested before being shipped out to assure perfect quality. I take pride in every one of my juggling props and I want my customers to feel that same pride.

Customer Comments

Here are a few select quotes from our happy family of customers and associates:

"I'm more than happy to recommend Dave Vinet's products. I came upon his work 10 years ago and was immediately impressed by his craftsmanship. He provides well-balanced and attractive props which are the perfect complement to my performances."

"Dave Vinet makes the best juggling equipment on the planet. Period."

"David hss been my main supplier for 20 years. I have never had a problem with his equipment and his service is impeccable."

THE J-PROP SHOP 541 WEST HIGHLAND DRIVE AUBURN, ME 04210 (207) 555 - 9001

Trouble? Many elements in HTML5 are still not completely supported in current browsers, so the appearance of your Web page might differ slightly from that shown in Figure 1-31. If you are running Internet Explorer 8 or earlier, you'll see a significant difference. You'll learn how to correct this problem shortly.

Using the new style sheet, Dave's Web page is much more readable. The page is displayed in a two-column layout with the main content of the section element displayed in the left column. The content of the aside element is shown as a sidebar in the right column with a light purple background, rounded corners, and a drop shadow. The content of the footer element is styled with a smaller font, a top border line, and a light purple background.

Styles for HTML5 Elements

The section, aside, and footer elements used in the code of the *jprop.htm* file are new HTML5 elements that were not part of earlier HTML specifications. For most browsers this is not a problem, and the Web page should be rendered with a format and layout close to what Dave requested. An important exception, though, is the Internet Explorer browser. Internet Explorer version 8 and earlier versions provide almost no support for HTML5 and do not recognize styles applied to HTML5 elements. For example, as Figure 1-32 shows, even with the new style sheet, Internet Explorer 8 displays Dave's Web page with a few of the styles shown in Figure 1-31.

Figure 1-32   **Web page as it appears in Internet Explorer 8**

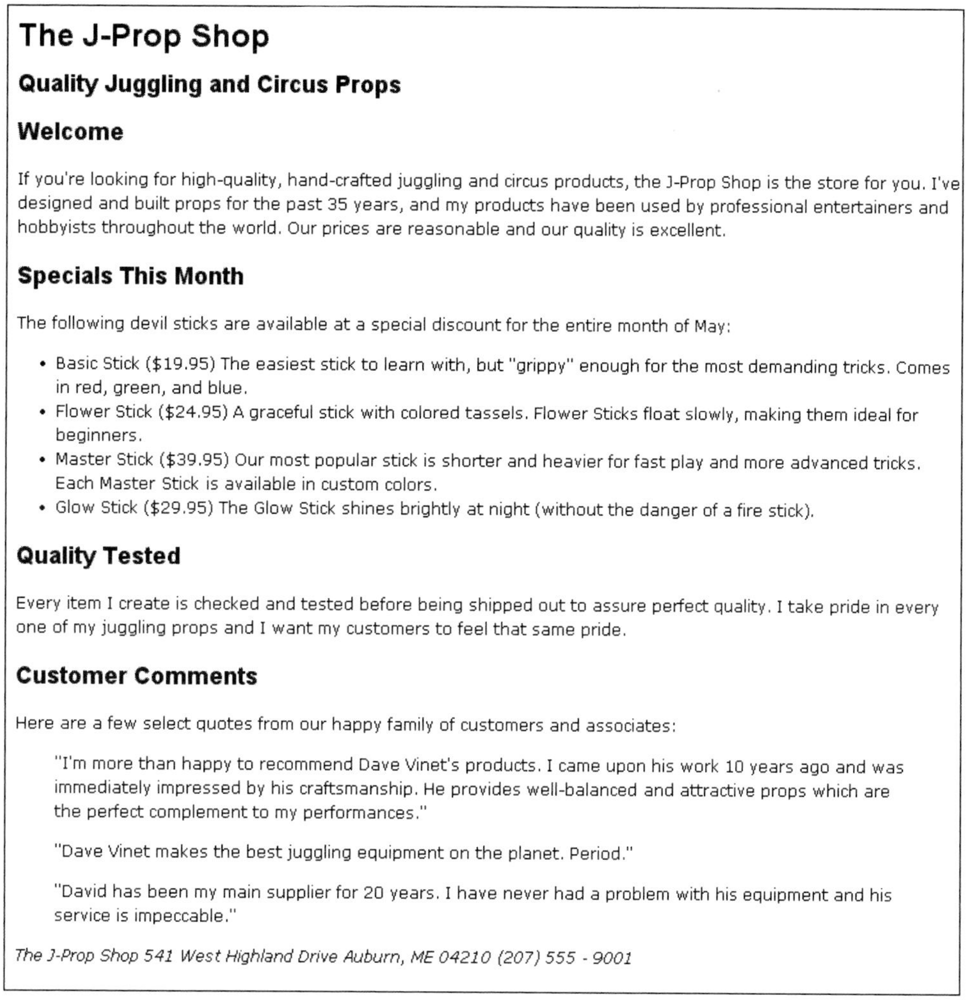

The J-Prop Shop

Quality Juggling and Circus Props

Welcome

If you're looking for high-quality, hand-crafted juggling and circus products, the J-Prop Shop is the store for you. I've designed and built props for the past 35 years, and my products have been used by professional entertainers and hobbyists throughout the world. Our prices are reasonable and our quality is excellent.

Specials This Month

The following devil sticks are available at a special discount for the entire month of May:

- Basic Stick ($19.95) The easiest stick to learn with, but "grippy" enough for the most demanding tricks. Comes in red, green, and blue.
- Flower Stick ($24.95) A graceful stick with colored tassels. Flower Sticks float slowly, making them ideal for beginners.
- Master Stick ($39.95) Our most popular stick is shorter and heavier for fast play and more advanced tricks. Each Master Stick is available in custom colors.
- Glow Stick ($29.95) The Glow Stick shines brightly at night (without the danger of a fire stick).

Quality Tested

Every item I create is checked and tested before being shipped out to assure perfect quality. I take pride in every one of my juggling props and I want my customers to feel that same pride.

Customer Comments

Here are a few select quotes from our happy family of customers and associates:

"I'm more than happy to recommend Dave Vinet's products. I came upon his work 10 years ago and was immediately impressed by his craftsmanship. He provides well-balanced and attractive props which are the perfect complement to my performances."

"Dave Vinet makes the best juggling equipment on the planet. Period."

"David has been my main supplier for 20 years. I have never had a problem with his equipment and his service is impeccable."

The J-Prop Shop 541 West Highland Drive Auburn, ME 04210 (207) 555 - 9001

Dave needs this problem fixed because he can't assume that users will always be running the latest version of Internet Explorer. Workarounds for this problem involve running an external program known as a **script**. The most often used program language for the Web is **JavaScript**. Like HTML and CSS files, JavaScript files are text files that require no special software other than a Web browser to run. At this point, you don't need to know how to write a JavaScript program to correct Internet Explorer's problem with HTML5 elements; someone else has already done that. You just need to know how to access and run their program.

One of the most useful programs to enable HTML5 support in older browsers is Modernizr. **Modernizr** is a free, open-source, MIT-licensed JavaScript library of functions that provides support for many HTML5 elements and for the newest CSS styles. One of the many uses of Modernizr is to enable support for HTML5 in older browsers. Modernizr is distributed in a single JavaScript file that you can download from *www.modernizr.com* and add to your Web site. To link a Web page to a JavaScript file, you add the `script` element

```
<script src="file"></script>
```

to the document head, where *file* is the name of the JavaScript file. The current version of Modernizr at the time of this writing is stored in the file *modernizr-1.5.js*. To link to this file, you add the following to the document head:

```
<script src="modernizr-1.5.js"></script>
```

The *modernizr-1.5.js* file has already been added to your data folder. Link to this file now to apply it to Dave's Web page.

To link to the Modernizr file:

1. Return to the **jprop.htm** file in your text editor.

2. Scroll to the top of the file and add the following tag pair above the `link` element, as shown in Figure 1-33:

   ```
   <script src="modernizr-1.5.js"></script>
   ```

Figure 1-33	Linking to the Modernizr script

```
<!DOCTYPE html>
<html>

   <head>
   <!-- The J-Prop Shop Sample Page
        Author: David Vinet
        Date:   3/1/2014
   -->
         <title>The J-Prop Shop</title>
         <script src="modernizr-1.5.js"></script>
         <link href="jpsstyles.css" rel="stylesheet" type="text/css" />
   </head>
```

Modernizr script file

3. Save your changes to the file.

4. If you have access to Internet Explorer 8, use that browser to open the **jprop.htm** file. As shown in Figure 1-34, the browser renders the Web page employing the page layout and many of the formats shown earlier in Figure 1-29.

Figure 1-34	Web page as it appears in Internet Explorer 8 with Modernizr

The J-Prop Shop
Quality Juggling and Circus Props

Welcome

If you're looking for high-quality, hand-crafted juggling and circus products, the J-Prop Shop is the store for you. I've designed and built props for the past 35 years, and my products have been used by professional entertainers and hobbyists throughout the world. Our prices are reasonable and our quality is excellent.

Specials This Month

The following devil sticks are available at a special discount for the entire month of May:

- Basic Stick ($19.95) The easiest stick to learn with, but "grippy" enough for the most demanding tricks. Comes in red, green, and blue.
- Flower Stick ($24.95) A graceful stick with colored tassels. Flower Sticks float slowly, making them ideal for beginners.
- Master Stick ($39.95) Our most popular stick is shorter and heavier for fast play and more advanced tricks. Each Master Stick is available in custom colors.
- Glow Stick ($29.95) The Glow Stick shines brightly at night (without the danger of a fire stick).

Quality Tested

Every item I create is checked and tested before being shipped out to assure perfect quality. I take pride in every one of my juggling props and I want my customers to feel that same pride.

Customer Comments

Here are a few select quotes from our happy family of customers and associates:

"I'm more than happy to recommend Dave Vinet's products. I came upon his work 10 years ago and was immediately impressed by his craftsmanship. He provides well-balanced and attractive props which are the perfect complement to my performances."

"Dave Vinet makes the best juggling equipment on the planet. Period."

"David has been my main supplier for 20 years. I have never had a problem with his equipment and his service is impeccable."

rounded corners and drop shadows are not supported in IE8

THE J-PROP SHOP 541 WEST HIGHLAND DRIVE AUBURN, ME 04210 (207) 555 - 9001

The rendering done by Internet Explorer 8 does not completely match what was shown under Internet Explorer 9 or many of the other competing browsers such as Firefox, Safari, or Google Chrome. For example, Internet Explorer 8 doesn't support styles for rounded corners and drop shadows. All of this underscores an important point: You may find variations between one browser and another in how your page is rendered, especially when using the newest HTML5 elements and CSS styles. This means you have to test your page under multiple browsers and devices, and make sure that any differences in format or layout do not impact your users' ability to read and understand your page.

Marking Text-Level Elements

Grouping elements like paragraphs and headings start their content on a new line. Another type of element is a **text-level element**, which marks content within a grouping element. A text-level element is like a phrase or a collection of characters within a paragraph or heading. Text-level elements do not start out on a new line, but instead flow alongside of, or **inline** with, the rest of the characters in the grouping element. Figure 1-35 lists some of the text-level elements in HTML.

Figure 1-35   **Text-level elements**

Text-Level Element	Description
a	A hypertext link
abbr	An abbreviation
b	Text offset from the surrounding content (usually displayed in **boldface** text)
cite	A citation (usually displayed in *italics*)
code	Program code (usually displayed in a `fixed width` font)
del	Deleted text (usually displayed with a ~~strikethrough~~ line)
dfn	A definition term (usually displayed in *italics*)
em	Emphasized content (usually displayed in *italics*)
i	Text representing an alternate voice or mood (usually displayed in *italics*)
ins	Inserted text (usually displayed with an <u>underline</u>)
kbd	Keyboard text (usually displayed in a `fixed width` font)
mark	Highlighted or marked text (usually displayed with a highlight. HTML5 only)
q	Quoted text (occasionally enclosed in "quotes")
samp	Sample computer code (usually displayed in a `fixed width` font)
small	Text displayed in a smaller font than surrounding content
span	A span of generic text
strong	Strongly emphasized content (usually displayed in **boldface** text)
sub	Subscripted text
sup	Superscripted text
time	A date and time value (HTML5 only)
var	Programming variables (usually displayed in *italic*)

TIP

Text-level elements should always be nested within grouping elements such as paragraphs or headings.

To practice using text-level elements in conjunction with grouping elements, you'll return to the HTML demo page.

To explore the use of inline elements:

1. Return to the **demo_html.htm** file in your Web browser.

2. Replace the code in the HTML Code box with the following:

   ```
   <p>Welcome to the J-Prop Shop, owned and operated by David
   Vinet</p>
   ```

3. Click the **Preview Code** button to display this paragraph in the Preview box.

   To mark *J-Prop Shop* as strongly emphasized text, you can enclose that phrase within a set of <strong> tags.

4. Insert the <strong> opening tag directly before the word *J-Prop* in the box on the left. Insert the closing </strong> tag directly after the word *Shop*. Click the **Preview Code** button to confirm that *J-Prop Shop* is now displayed in a bold-faced font.

   Another text-level element is the cite element used to make citations. Explore how citations are rendered by your browser by enclosing *David Vinet* within a set of <cite> tags.

5. Insert an opening <cite> tag directly before the word *David* and insert the closing </cite> tag directly after *Vinet*. Click the **Preview Code** button to view the revised code. Figure 1-36 shows the result of applying the <strong> and <cite> tags to the paragraph text.

Figure 1-36 Applying the strong and cite text-level elements

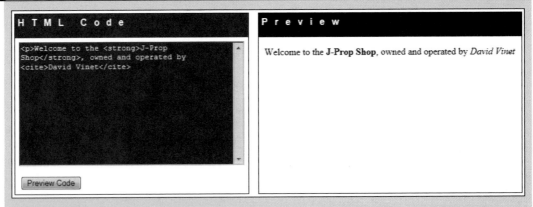

6. Continue exploring other HTML elements listed in Figure 1-35 to see their effects on the rendered text. Close the demo file when you're done.

You can nest text-level tags to mark a single text string with more than one element. For example, the HTML code

```
<p>Welcome to the <strong><em>J-Prop Shop</em></strong>.</p>
```

marks the text string *J-Prop Shop* as both strong and emphasized text. In most browsers it appears in a ***bold italic*** font.

Dave wants the names of all of the items in his product list to be marked as strong text. Revise the code for the product names now.

To mark strong text:

▶ **1.** Return to the **jprop.htm** file in your text editor.

▶ **2.** Scroll down to the unordered list and enclose the name and price of each product within a set of **<strong>** tags as shown in Figure 1-37.

Figure 1-37 | **Marking product names using the strong element**

```
<article>
    <h2>Specials This Month</h2>
    <p>The following devil sticks are available at a
        special discount for the entire month of May:
    </p>

    <ul>
        <li><strong>Basic Stick ($19.95)</strong>
            The easiest stick to learn with, but "grippy" enough
            for the most demanding tricks. Comes in red, green,
            and blue.
        </li>
        <li><strong>Flower Stick ($24.95)</strong>
            A graceful stick with colored tassels. Flower Sticks
            float slowly, making them ideal for beginners.
        </li>
        <li><strong>Master Stick ($39.95)</strong>
            Our most popular stick is shorter and heavier for
            fast play and more advanced tricks. Each Master Stick
            is available in custom colors.
        </li>
        <li><strong>Glow Stick ($29.95)</strong>
            The Glow Stick shines brightly at night (without
            the danger of a fire stick).
        </li>
    </ul>

</article>
```

▶ **3.** Save your changes to the file and then reload the **jprop.htm** file in your Web browser. Figure 1-38 shows the revised appearance of the bulleted list of products.

Figure 1-38 | **Product names rendered in a boldfaced font**

Specials This Month

The following devil sticks are available at a special discount for the entire month of May:

- **Basic Stick ($19.95)** The easiest stick to learn with, but "grippy" enough for the most demanding tricks. Comes in red, green, and blue.
- **Flower Stick ($24.95)** A graceful stick with colored tassels. Flower Sticks float slowly, making them ideal for beginners.
- **Master Stick ($39.95)** Our most popular stick is shorter and heavier for fast play and more advanced tricks. Each Master Stick is available in custom colors.
- **Glow Stick ($29.95)** The Glow Stick shines brightly at night (without the danger of a fire stick).

Written Communication: Logical and Physical Interpretation of Elements

As you learn more HTML, you'll notice some overlap in how browsers display certain elements. To display italicized text, you could use the <dfn>, <em>, <i>, or <var> tags; or if you wanted to italicize an entire block of text, you could use the <address> tag. However, browsers differ in how they display elements, so you should not rely on the way any browser or group of browsers commonly displays an element.

In addition, it's important to distinguish between the way a browser displays an element, and the purpose of the element in the document. Although it can be tempting to ignore this difference, your HTML code benefits when you respect that distinction because search engines often look within specific elements for information. For example, a search engine may look for the address element to find contact information for a particular Web site. It would be confusing to end users if you used the address element to simply italicize a block of text. Web programmers can also use elements to extract information from a page. For example, a JavaScript program could automatically generate a bibliography from all of the citations listed within a Web site by looking for occurrences of the cite element.

The best practice for communicating the purpose of your document is to use HTML to mark content but not to rely on HTML to format that content. Formatting should be done solely through style sheets, using either the internal style sheets built into browsers or through your own customized styles.

Using the Generic Elements div and span

Most of the page elements you've examined have a specific meaning. However, sometimes you want to add an element that represents a text block or a string of inline text without it having any other meaning. HTML supports two such generic elements: div and span. The div element is used to mark general grouping content and has the following syntax:

```
<div>content</div>
```

The span element, which is used to mark general text-level content, has the following syntax:

```
<span>content</span>
```

Browsers recognize both elements but do not assign any default format to content marked with these elements. This frees Web authors to develop styles for these elements without worrying about overriding any styles imposed by browsers. Note that the main use of the div element to mark sections of the page has been superseded in HTML5 by the sectional elements such as header and article; however, you will still encounter the div element in many current and older Web sites.

INSIGHT

Presentational Attributes

Early versions of HTML were used mostly by scientists and researchers who, for the most part, didn't need flashy graphics, decorative text fonts, or even much color on a page. The earliest Web pages weren't fancy and didn't require much from the browsers that displayed them. This changed as the Web became more popular and attracted the attention of commercial businesses, graphic designers, and artists.

One way that HTML changed to accommodate this new class of users was to introduce **presentational elements** and **presentational attributes** designed to describe how each element should be rendered by Web browsers. For example, to align text on a page, Web authors would use the `align` attribute

```
<element align="alignment">content</element>
```

where *alignment* is either *left*, *right*, *center*, or *justify*. Thus, to center an `h1` heading on a page, you could apply the following `align` attribute to the `<h1>` tag:

```
<h1 align="center">The J-Prop Shop</h1>
```

Almost all presentational elements and attributes are now deprecated in favor of style sheets, but you may still see them used in older Web sites. Using a deprecated attribute like `align` would probably not cause a Web page to fail, but it's still best to focus your HTML code on describing the content of a document and not its appearance.

Marking a Line Break

After examining your work, Dave notices that the list of customer comments lacks the names of the customers who made them. He asks you to add this information to the Web page, marking the customer information as citations.

To append customer names to the Customer Comments section:

1. Return to the **jprop.htm** file in your text editor.

2. Locate the first customer comment and then add the following code at the end of the paragraph, directly before the closing `</p>` tag:

```
<cite>Thomas Gage, Circus England</cite>
```

3. At the end of the paragraph for the second customer comment, insert

```
<cite>Douglas Pederson, Street-Wise Shows</cite>
```

4. Finally, at the end of the paragraph for the third customer comment, insert

```
<cite>Linda Unger, Linda & Louis</cite>
```

Figure 1-39 shows the revised code in the file.

| Figure 1-39 | Providing citations for the customer quotes |

```
<aside>
   <h2>Customer Comments</h2>
   <p>Here are a few select quotes from our happy family
      of customers and associates:
   </p>
   <blockquote>
      <p>"I'm more than happy to recommend Dave Vinet's
         products. I came upon his work 10 years ago and
         was immediately impressed by his craftsmanship.
         He provides well-balanced and attractive
         props which are the perfect complement to my
         performances."
         <cite>Thomas Gage, Circus England</cite>
      </p>
      <p>"Dave Vinet makes the best juggling equipment on
         the planet. Period."
         <cite>Douglas Pederson, Street-Wise Shows</cite>
      </p>
      <p>"David has been my main supplier for 20 years. I
         have never had a problem with his equipment and
         his service is impeccable."
         <cite>Linda Unger, Linda & Louis</cite>
      </p>
   </blockquote>
</aside>
```

5. Save your changes to the file and then refresh the **jprop.htm** file in your Web browser. Figure 1-40 shows the revised text of the Customer Comments sidebar.

| Figure 1-40 | Revised Customer Comments sidebar |

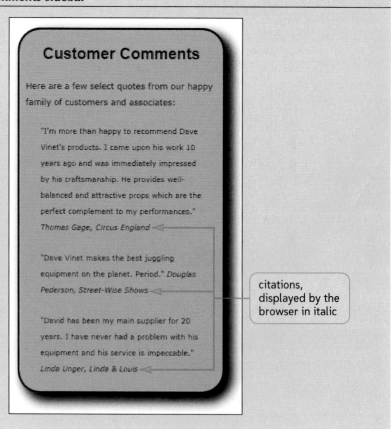

citations, displayed by the browser in italic

Dave thinks the comments are difficult to read when the text of a comment runs into the citation. He suggests that you start each citation on a new line. To do this, you can insert a line break into the Web page using the following empty element tag:

```
<br />
```

Line breaks must be placed within grouping elements such as paragraphs or headings. Some browsers accept line breaks placed anywhere within the body of a Web page; however, this is not good coding technique. A browser displaying an XHTML document will reject code in which a text-level element such as `br` is placed outside of any grouping element.

You'll use the `br` element to mark a line break between each customer comment and its associated citation in Dave's Web page.

To insert line breaks in the comments:

1. Return to the **jprop.htm** file in your text editor.

2. Insert the tag **
** between the comment and the citation for each of the three customer comments in the file. See Figure 1-41.

Figure 1-41 | **Inserting line breaks**

line break element

```
<blockquote>
    <p>"I'm more than happy to recommend Dave Vinet's
        products. I came upon his work 10 years ago and
        was immediately impressed by his craftsmanship.
        He provides well-balanced and attractive
        props which are the perfect complement to my
        performances."
        <br />
        <cite>Thomas Gage, Circus England</cite>
    </p>
    <p>"Dave Vinet makes the best juggling equipment on
        the planet. Period."
        <br />
        <cite>Douglas Pederson, Street-Wise Shows</cite>
    </p>
    <p>"David has been my main supplier for 20 years. I
        have never had a problem with his equipment and
        his service is impeccable."
        <br />
        <cite>Linda Unger, Linda & Louis</cite>
    </p>
</blockquote>
```

3. Save your changes to the file and then refresh the **jprop.htm** file in your Web browser. Verify that each citation starts on a new line below the associated customer comment.

Marking a Horizontal Rule

INSIGHT

Another empty element is `hr`, the horizontal rule element, which marks a major topic change within a section. The syntax of the `hr` element is as follows:

```
<hr />
```

The exact appearance of the `hr` element is left to the browser. Most browsers display a gray-shaded horizontal line a few pixels in height. The `hr` element was originally used as a quick way of inserting horizontal lines within a Web page. Although that task now should be left to style sheets, you will still see the `hr` element in older Web pages.

Inserting an Inline Image

Dave wants you to replace the name of the company at the top of his Web page with an image of the company logo. Because HTML files are simple text files, non-textual content such as graphics must be stored in separate files, which are then loaded by browsers as they render pages. To add a graphic image to a Web page, you have to insert an inline image into your code.

The `img` Element

Inline images are inserted into a Web page using the one-sided `img` element with the syntax

```
<img src="file" alt="text" />
```

where *file* is the name of the graphic image file and *text* is text displayed by browsers in place of the graphic image. In this tutorial, you'll assume that the graphic image file is located in the same folder as the Web page, so you don't have to specify the location of the file. In the next tutorial, you'll learn how to reference files placed in other folders or locations on the Web.

Browsers retrieve the specified image file and display the image alongside the rest of the Web page content. The size of the image is based on the dimensions of the image itself; however, you can specify a different size using the `width` and `height` attributes

```
width="value" height="value"
```

where the width and height values are expressed in pixels. If you specify only the width, browsers automatically set the height to maintain the proportions of the image; similarly, if you define the height, browsers automatically set the width to maintain the image proportions. Thus, by setting the width and height values yourself, you can enlarge or reduce the size of the rendered image.

Inline images are considered text-level elements and thus must be placed within a grouping element such as a heading or a paragraph. An inline image is most commonly stored in one of three formats: GIF (Graphics Interchange Format), JPEG (Joint Photographic Experts Group), or PNG (Portable Network Graphics). Dave has already created his graphic image in PNG format and stored it with his other files using the filename *jpslogo.png*. You'll replace the text of the `h1` heading with this inline image.

To insert the company logo at the top of the page:

1. Return to the **jprop.htm** file in your text editor.

2. Go to the `h1` heading element at the top of the body section, delete the text *The J-Prop Shop* from between the opening and closing `<h1>` tags, and then replace it with

   ```
   <img src="jpslogo.png" alt="The J-Prop Shop" />
   ```

   Figure 1-42 highlights the revised code in the **jprop.htm** file.

Figure 1-42 | Adding an inline image

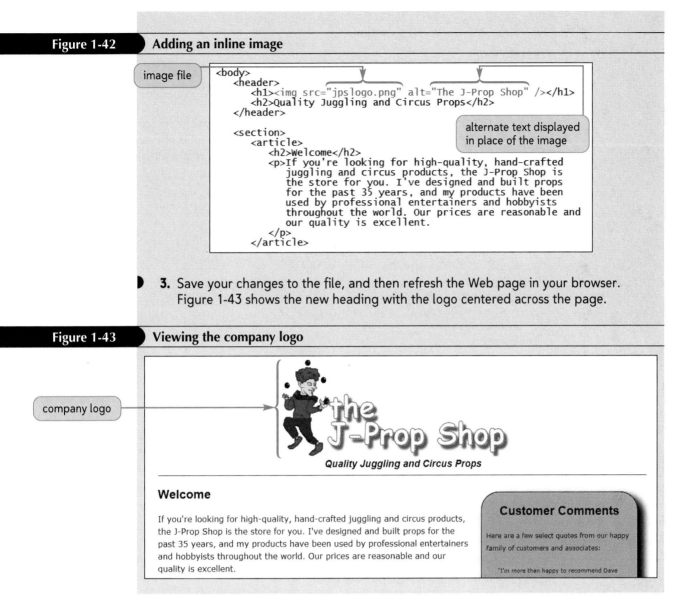

3. Save your changes to the file, and then refresh the Web page in your browser. Figure 1-43 shows the new heading with the logo centered across the page.

Figure 1-43 | Viewing the company logo

Figures and Figure Captions

In books and magazines, figures and figure captions are often placed within boxes that stand aside from the main content of an article. HTML5 introduced this type of object to Web page markup with the `figure` and `figcaption` elements

```
<figure>
   content
   <figcaption>caption</figcaption>
</figure>
```

where *content* is the content that will appear in the figure box and *caption* is the text of the figure caption. The `figcaption` element is optional; but if the `figcaption` element is used, it must be nested within a set of `<figure>` tags either directly after the opening `<figure>` tag or directly before the closing `</figure>` tag. For example, the following HTML5 code creates a figure box containing an inline image of one of the J-Prop Shop's products and a caption:

```
<figure>
    <img src="stick03.png" alt="Master Stick" />
    <figcaption>Master Stick ($39.95)</figcaption>
</figure>
```

The `figure` element doesn't necessarily need to contain an inline image. It can be used to mark any content that stands aside from a main article but is referenced by it. For instance, it could be used to contain an excerpt of a poem, as the following code demonstrates:

```
<figure>
    <p>'Twas brillig, and the slithy toves<br />
        Did gyre and gimble in the wabe;<br />
        All mimsy were the borogoves,<br />
        And the mome raths outgrabe.
    </p>
    <figcaption>
        <cite>Jabberwocky,
        Lewis Carroll, 1832-98</cite>
    </figcaption>
</figure>
```

As with other HTML elements, the exact appearance of a figure box is determined by a style sheet. At this time, Dave does not need to create a figure box for his company's home page.

Working with Character Sets and Special Characters

Dave likes the work you've done so far on the Web page. He has only one remaining concern: The company's address in the page footer is difficult to read because the street address, city name, zip code, and phone number all run together on one line. Dave would like to have the different parts of the address separated by a solid circular marker (•). However, this marker is not represented by any keys on your keyboard. How, then, do you insert this symbol into the Web page?

Character Sets

Every character that your browser is capable of rendering belongs to a collection of characters and symbols called a **character set**. Character sets come in a wide variety of sizes. For English, no more than about 127 characters are needed to represent all of the upper- and lowercase letters, numbers, punctuation marks, spaces, and special typing symbols in the language. Other languages, such as Japanese or Chinese, require character sets containing thousands of symbols. Beyond the basic characters used by a language are special characters such as ©, ½, π, and ®. Thus, a complete character set that includes all possible printable characters is made up of hundreds of symbols.

The character set used for the alphabet of English characters is called **ASCII (American Standard Code for Information Interchange)**. A more extended character set, called **Latin-1** or the **ISO 8859-1** character set, supports 255 characters and can be used by most languages that employ the Latin alphabet, including English, French, Spanish, and Italian. **Unicode**, the most extended character set, supports up to 65,536 symbols and can be used for any of the world's languages. The most commonly used character set on the Web is **UTF-8**, which is a compressed version of Unicode and is probably the default character set assumed by your browser. You can learn more about character sets by visiting the W3C Web site and the Web site for the Internet Assigned Numbers Authority at *www.iana.org*.

Character Encoding

Character encoding associates each symbol from a character set with a numeric value called the **numeric character reference**. For example, the copyright symbol © from the UTF-8 character set is encoded with the number 169. If you know the character encoding number, you can insert the corresponding character directly into your Web page using the entity

    &#code;

where *code* is the encoding number. Thus, to display the © symbol in your Web page, you would enter

    ©

into your HTML file.

Character Entity References

Another way to insert a special symbol is to use a **character entity reference**, which is a short memorable name used in place of the encoding number. Character entity references are inserted using the syntax

    &char;

where *char* is the character's entity reference. The character entity reference for the copyright symbol is *copy*. So to display the © symbol in your Web page, you could insert

    ©

into your HTML code.

REFERENCE

Inserting Symbols from a Character Set

- To insert a symbol based on the encoding number, use the entity
  `&#code;`
  where *code* is the encoding number.
- To insert a symbol based on a character entity reference, use the entity
  `&char;`
  where *char* is the name assigned to the character.
- To insert a nonbreaking space, use the following entity:
  ` `
- To insert the < symbol, use the following entity:
  `&lt;`
- To insert the > symbol, use the following entity:
  `&gt;`

You can explore various encoding numbers and character entity references by opening the demo page supplied with your Data Files.

To view the demo page:

1. Use your Web browser to open the **demo_characters.htm** file from the tutorial.01\demo data folder.

2. Type `&#163;` in the input box and then click the **Show** button. The Web browser displays the £ symbol in the ivory-colored box below.

3. Replace the value in the input box with ® and then click the **Show** button. The browser now displays the ® symbol, the symbol for registered trademarks, which you specified using a character entity reference.

You can also view a collection of numeric character references and character entity references by selecting a table from the list box on the page.

4. Verify that General Symbols is displayed in the selection list box, and then click the **Show Table** button. As shown in Figure 1-44, the browser displays a list of 35 symbols with the character entity reference and the numeric character reference displayed beneath each symbol.

Figure 1-44	HTML characters demo page

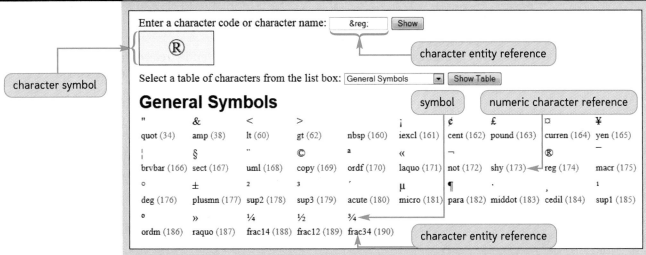

5. Take some time to explore the variety of numeric character references and character entity references supported by your browser. Close the demo page when you're finished, but leave your browser open.

Special Characters

One use of character codes is to insert text about HTML itself. For example, if you want your Web page to describe the use of the <h1> tag, you cannot simply type

```
The <h1> tag is used to mark h1 headings.
```

because browsers would interpret the <h1> text as marking the beginning of an h1 heading! Instead, you have to use the < and > entity references to insert the < and > symbols. The text would then be:

```
The &lt;h1&gt; tag is used to mark h1 headings.
```

Another use of character codes is to add extra spaces to your Web page. Remember that browsers ignore extra blank spaces in an HTML file. To insert an additional space, use the   entity reference (*nbsp* stands for *nonbreaking space*), which forces browsers to insert an extra space.

On Dave's Web page, you decide to use the bullet symbol (•) to break up the address text into sections. The symbol has a character encoding number of 8226 and the character entity reference name *bull*. Dave suggests that you also add a long horizontal line known as an em-dash (—) to mark the customer names in the customer comments section. The character encoding number for an em-dash is 8212 and the entity reference is *mdash*.

To add bullets and an em-dash to Dave's Web page:

1. Return to the **jprop.htm** file in your text editor.

2. Locate the customer comment from Thomas Gage, and then directly before the opening <cite> tag insert the character code — followed by a space.

3. Repeat Step 2 for the two remaining customer comments.

Always include a semi-colon so that browsers recognize the entry as a character code.

4. Scroll down to the address element within the page footer. At the end of each line within the address (except the last line), insert a space followed by the • character entity. Figure 1-45 highlights the revised code in the Web page.

Figure 1-45	Adding symbols from a character set

```
<aside>
    <h2>Customer Comments</h2>
    <p>Here are a few select quotes from our happy family
        of customers and associates:
    </p>
    <blockquote>
        <p>"I'm more than happy to recommend Dave Vinet's
            products. I came upon his work 10 years ago and
            was immediately impressed by his craftsmanship.
            He provides well-balanced and attractive
            props which are the perfect complement to my
            performances."
            <br />
            &#8212; <cite>Thomas Gage, Circus England</cite>
        </p>
        <p>"Dave Vinet makes the best juggling equipment on
            the planet. Period."
            <br />
            &#8212; <cite>Douglas Pederson, Street-Wise Shows</cite>
        </p>
        <p>"David has been my main supplier for 20 years. I
            have never had a problem with his equipment and
            his service is impeccable."
            <br />
            &#8212; <cite>Linda Unger, Linda & Louis</cite>
        </p>
    </blockquote>
</aside>

<footer>
    <address>The J-Prop Shop &bull;
             541 West Highland Drive &bull;
             Auburn, ME 04210 &bull;
             (207) 555 - 9001
    </address>
</footer>
</body>
```

character encoding number → —

character entity reference → •

5. Save your changes to the file.

6. Refresh the **jprop.htm** file in your Web browser. Figure 1-46 shows the final content of Dave's Web page.

Figure 1-46   **Completed Web page**

Quality Juggling and Circus Props

Welcome

If you're looking for high-quality, hand-crafted juggling and circus products, the J-Prop Shop is the store for you. I've designed and built props for the past 35 years, and my products have been used by professional entertainers and hobbyists throughout the world. Our prices are reasonable and our quality is excellent.

Specials This Month

The following devil sticks are available at a special discount for the entire month of May:

- **Basic Stick ($19.95)** The easiest stick to learn with, but "grippy" enough for the most demanding tricks. Comes in red, green, and blue.
- **Flower Stick ($24.95)** A graceful stick with colored tassels. Flower Sticks float slowly, making them ideal for beginners.
- **Master Stick ($39.95)** Our most popular stick is shorter and heavier for fast play and more advanced tricks. Each Master Stick is available in custom colors.
- **Glow Stick ($29.95)** The Glow Stick shines brightly at night (without the danger of a fire stick).

Quality Tested

Every item I create is checked and tested before being shipped out to assure perfect quality. I take pride in every one of my juggling props and I want my customers to feel that same pride.

Customer Comments

Here are a few select quotes from our happy family of customers and associates:

"I'm more than happy to recommend Dave Vinet's products. I came upon his work 10 years ago and was immediately impressed by his craftsmanship. He provides well-balanced and attractive props which are the perfect complement to my performances."
— Thomas Gage, Circus England

"Dave Vinet makes the best juggling equipment on the planet. Period."
— Douglas Federson, Street-Wise Shows

"David has been my main supplier for 20 years. I have never had a problem with his equipment and his service is impeccable."
— Linda Unger, Linda & Louis

THE J-PROP SHOP • 541 WEST HIGHLAND DRIVE • AUBURN, ME 04210 • (207) 555 - 9001

Specifying the Character Set

To render a numeric character reference correctly, a browser must apply the correct character set to a Web page. This information is typically sent by the Web server as it transfers an HTML page to a browser. However, to be doubly certain that browsers employ the correct character set, you can specify the character set within the head element of your HTML document. For HTML 4.01 and XHTML, you add the meta element

```
<meta http-equiv="Content-Type"
      content="text/html; charset=character_set" />
```

to the document head, where `character_set` is the name of the character set you want the browser to employ when interpreting your HTML code. Under HTML5, the `meta` element is simply:

```
<meta charset="character_set" />
```

> **TIP**
>
> The `meta` element is also used to store information and keywords describing a document and its purpose.

HTML5 also supports the syntax of the HTML 4.01 and XHTML `meta` element. You should always specify the character encoding in your document, even if you are not using any special symbols. It relieves the browser from having to guess about the correct encoding; and in certain situations, not specifying the encoding can lead to a security hole in the transfer of a page from the Web server to the client.

You'll add the `meta` element to Dave's document to specify that his file has been encoded using the UTF-8 character set.

To specify the character encoding for Dave's document:

1. Return to the **jprop.htm** file in your text editor.
2. Scroll to the top of the file. Directly below the comment in the head section, insert the following `meta` element as shown in Figure 1-47:

   ```
   <meta charset="UTF-8" />
   ```

Figure 1-47 Specifying the character encoding

```
<!DOCTYPE html>
<html>

   <head>
      <!-- The J-Prop Shop Sample Page
           Author: David Vinet
           Date:   3/1/2014
      -->
      <meta charset="UTF-8" />
      <title>The J-Prop Shop</title>
      <script src="modernizr-1.5.js"></script>
      <link href="jpsstyles.css" rel="stylesheet" type="text/css" />
   </head>
```

character set

3. Close the **jprop.htm** file, saving your changes.
4. Refresh the **jprop.htm** file in your browser and verify that the browser renders the page with no errors.

PROSKILLS

Written Communication: Publishing Your Web Page

Once you've completed your Web page, your next step is to get it on the Web. You first need to find a Web server to host the page. In choosing a Web server, you'll need to consider how much you want to pay, how much space you need, and how much traffic you expect at your Web site. If you'd prefer a free or low-cost option and don't need much space, you might first look toward the company that provides your Internet access. Most **Internet service providers** (ISPs) offer space on their Web servers as part of their regular service or for a small fee. However, they usually limit the amount of space available to you, unless you pay an extra fee to host a larger site. There are also free Web hosts, which provide space on servers for personal or noncommercial use. Once again, the amount of space you get is limited. Free Web hosting services make their money from selling advertising space on your site, so you should be prepared to act as a billboard in return for space on their servers. Finally, you can pay a monthly fee to an ISP to host your Web site to get more space and bandwidth.

Once you identify a Web host, you next need to consider the domain name that identifies your site. If you're planning to create a commercial site to advertise a product or service, you'll want the domain name to reflect your business. Free Web hosts usually include their names in your Web address. Thus, instead of having a Web address like

thejpropshop.com

you might have something like

freewebhosting.net/members/thejpropshop.html

If you're running a site for personal use, this might not be a problem—but it would look unprofessional on a commercial site. If you are planning a commercial site and simply want to advertise your product by publishing an online brochure, you can usually find an inexpensive host and pay a nominal yearly fee to reserve a Web address that reflects your company's name.

REVIEW

Session 1.2 Quick Check

1. Specify the code you would enter to mark the text *The J-Prop Shop* as an `h1` heading and the text *Product List* as an `h2` heading. Add code to group these two headings so browsers recognize them as a heading and subheading, respectively.

2. Specify the code you would enter to mark the text *Hamlet by William Shakespeare* as an `h1` heading, with a line break after the word *Hamlet*.

3. Create an ordered list of the following items: Packers, Bears, Lions, Vikings.

4. Specify the code to access the CSS style sheet file *uwstyles.css*. Where should you place this code within an HTML file?

5. Mark the graphic file *portrait.gif* as an inline image, setting the dimensions to 250 pixels wide by 300 pixels high. Specify the text *David Vinet* as alternate text to be displayed in place of the image for non-graphical browsers.

6. Specify the code to place the *portrait.gif* image from the previous question within a figure box with the caption *David Vinet, owner of the J-Prop Shop*.

7. The trademark symbol (™) has the character encoding number 8482. Provide the HTML code to enter this symbol into your Web page.

8. The Greek letter ß has the character entity name *beta*. How would you enter this symbol into your Web page?

Review Assignments

Data Files needed for the Review Assignments: basiclogo.png, basicstick.png, basicstyles.css, modernizr-1.5.js, stick.txt

Dave has found a host for his Web page and has published the document you helped him create on the Internet. Now he wants to start adding more pages to his Web site. He's come to you for help in creating a page describing his basic stick. He's already written the text for the Web page; he needs you to mark up that text with HTML code. Figure 1-48 shows a preview of the page you'll create for Dave.

Figure 1-48	The Basic Stick product page

Specials This Month

The Basic Stick

The Basic Stick is the perfect stick for beginners. The stick rotates slowly to provide extra time for performing stick tricks, but is flashy enough to impress your friends. Enjoy the following:

Our Basic Stick

Patented Dura-Coat® finish ensures sticks can withstand all weather conditions. More durable than other sticks, these props will keep looking like new for as long as you own them.

Enhanced stick flexibility provides more bounce, allowing for better tricks. A soft rubber core adds a whole new element to the sticking experience that you have to feel to believe!

Full customization will give you the chance to own a pair of sticks unlike any others out there. I make exactly what you want, with your colors and your designs.

A personal touch through both my customization options and hand-crafted designs.

Specifications

- Main Stick
  - Weight: 7 oz.
  - Length: 24 inches
  - Tape: Dura-Coat® finish with laser-style color choices
- Handle Sticks (one pair)
  - Weight: 2 oz.
  - Length: 18 inches
  - Tape: Soft ivory tape with rubber core

THE J-PROP SHOP ♦ 541 WEST HIGHLAND DRIVE ♦ AUBURN, ME 04210 ♦ (207) 555 - 9001

Complete the following:

1. Use your text editor to create a new file named **basic.htm**, and then save it in the tutorial.01\review folder included with your Data Files.
2. Add the doctype for an HTML5 document.
3. Create the root `html` element and nest the `head` and `body` elements within it.

4. Within the `head` element, insert the comment

   ```
   The J-Prop Shop
   Sample Page for the Basic Stick
   Author: your name
   Date:   the date
   ```

   where *your name* is your name and *the date* is the current date.

5. Add code to specify that the page uses the UTF-8 character set.

6. Set the page title as **Basic Sticks**.

7. Link the file to the **modernizr-1.5.js** script file to enable HTML5 support for older browsers.

8. Link the file to the **basicstyles.css** style sheet file.

9. Within the `body` element, create structural elements for the page header, main section, and footer.

10. Within the page header, insert an `h1` heading containing the inline image file **basiclogo.png**. Specify the following alternate text for the image: **The J-Prop Shop**. Below the `h1` heading, insert an `h2` heading containing the text **Specials This Month**. Group the `h1` and `h2` headings using the `hgroup` element.

11. Within the `section` element, insert an `aside` element. The `aside` element should contain an inline image pointing to the *basicstick.png* file and having the text string **photo** as the alternate text. Below the inline image within the `aside` element, insert a paragraph containing the text string **Our Basic Stick**.

12. Add two `article` elements to the `section` element.

13. Within the first article, insert an `h2` heading containing the text **The Basic Stick**. Add a paragraph containing the following text:

    The Basic Stick is the perfect stick for beginners. The stick rotates slowly to provide extra time for performing stick tricks, but is flashy enough to impress your friends. Enjoy the following:

14. Add a block quote containing the following four paragraphs (you can copy this text from the *stick.txt* file):

    Patented Dura-Coat finish ensures sticks can withstand all weather conditions. More durable than other sticks, these props will keep looking like new for as long as you own them.

    Enhanced stick flexibility provides more bounce, allowing for better tricks. A soft rubber core adds a whole new element to the sticking experience that you have to feel to believe!

    Full customization will give you the chance to own a pair of sticks unlike any others out there. I make exactly what you want, with your colors and your designs.

    A personal touch through both my customization options and hand-crafted designs.

15. Mark the first few words of each of the four paragraphs as strong text, as shown in Figure 1-48.

16. Within the second article element, insert an `h2` heading with the title **Specifications**.

17. Directly below the `h2` heading, insert an unordered list. The list should contain two items: **Main Stick** and **Handle Sticks (one pair)**.

18. Within the *Main Stick* list item, insert a nested unordered list containing the following items:
    - **Weight: 7 oz.**
    - **Length: 24 inches**
    - **Tape: Dura-Coat finish with laser-style color choices**

19. Within the *Handle Sticks (one pair)* list item, insert a nested unordered list containing the following items:
    - **Weight: 2 oz.**
    - **Length: 18 inches**
    - **Tape: Soft ivory tape with rubber core**

20. Locate the two occurrences of *Dura-Coat* in the document. Directly after the word *Dura-Coat*, insert the registered trademark symbol ®. The character entity name of the ® symbol is *reg*. Display the ® symbol as a superscript by placing the character within the sup element.

21. Within the page footer, insert the company's address:

    The J-Prop Shop
    541 West Highland Drive
    Auburn, ME 04210
    (207) 555 - 9001

22. Separate the different sections of the address using a solid diamond (character code 9830).

23. Save your changes to the file, open it in your Web browser, and then compare your Web page to Figure 1-48 to verify that it was rendered correctly. Older browsers may display some slight differences in the design.

24. Submit your completed files to your instructor, in either printed or electronic form, as requested.

Apply your knowledge of HTML5 to create a Web page for a mathematics Web site.

APPLY

Case Problem 1

Data Files needed for the Case Problem: mhlogo.jpg, mhstyles.css, mhtxt.htm, modernizr-1.5.js

Math High   Professor Lauren Coe of the Mathematics Department of Coastal University in Anderson, South Carolina, is one of the founders of *Math High*, a Web site containing articles and course materials for high school and college math instructors. She has written a series of biographies of famous mathematicians for the Web site and would like you to transfer content she's already written to an HTML5 file. You'll create the first one in this exercise. Figure 1-49 shows a preview of the page you'll create, which profiles the mathematician Leonhard Euler.

Figure 1-49	Math High Web page

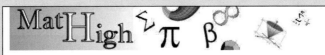

Leonhard Euler (1707-1783)

The greatest mathematician of the eighteenth century, **Leonhard Euler** was born in Basel, Switzerland. There, he studied under another giant of mathematics, **Jean Bernoulli**. In 1731 Euler became a professor of physics and mathematics at St. Petersburg Academy of Sciences. Euler was the most prolific mathematician of all time, publishing over *800 different books and papers*. His influence was felt in physics and astronomy as well.

He is perhaps best known for his research into mathematical analysis. Euler's work, *Introductio in analysin infinitorum (1748)*, remained a standard textbook in the field for well over a century. For the princess of Anhalt-Dessau he wrote *Lettres à une princesse d'Allemagne (1768-1772)*, giving a clear non-technical outline of the main physical theories of the time.

One can hardly write a mathematical equation without copying Euler. Notations still in use today, such as *e* and π, were introduced in Euler's writings. Leonhard Euler died in 1783, leaving behind a legacy perhaps unmatched, and certainly unsurpassed, in the annals of mathematics.

The Most Beautiful Theorem?

Euler's Equation:

$$\cos(x) + i\sin(x) = e^{\,(ix)}$$

demonstrates the relationship between algebra, complex analysis, and trigonometry. From this equation, it's easy to derive the identity:

$$e^{\,(\pi i)} + 1 = 0$$

which relates the fundamental constants: 0, 1, π, *e*, and *i* in a single beautiful and elegant statement. A poll of readers conducted by *The Mathematical Intelligencer* magazine named Euler's Identity as the most beautiful theorem in the history of mathematics.

MATH HIGH: A SITE FOR EDUCATORS AND RESEARCHERS

Complete the following:

1. In your text editor, open the **mhtxt.htm** file from the tutorial.01\case1 folder included with your Data Files. Save the file as **mathhigh.htm** in the same folder.

2. Enclose the contents of the file within a set of opening and closing `<html>` tags. Set the doctype of the file to indicate that this is an HTML5 document.

3. Add `head` and `body` elements to the file, enclosing the page contents within the body element.

4. Within the document head, insert the comment

   Math High: Leonhard Euler

   Author: *your name*

   Date: *the date*

   where *your name* is your name and *the date* is the current date.

5. Set the character set of the document to **UTF-8**.

6. Add the page title **Math High: Leonhard Euler** to the document head.

7. Link to the **modernizr-1.5.js** script file.

8. Link to the **mhstyles.css** style sheet.

9. Within the page body, create a `header` element. Within this element, insert an inline image using the **mhlogo.jpg** file as the source and **Math High** as the alternate text.

10. Mark the page text from the line *Leonhard Euler (1707 - 1783)* up to (but not including) the line *The Most Beautiful Theorem?* as an article.

11. Mark the first line in the article element, containing *Leonhard Euler (1707 - 1783)*, as an `h1` heading.

12. Mark the next three blocks of text describing Euler's life as paragraphs.

13. Within the first paragraph, mark the names *Leonhard Euler* and *Jean Bernoulli* using the `strong` element. Mark the phrase *800 different books and papers* as emphasized text using the `em` element.

14. In the second paragraph, mark the phrase *Introductio in analysin infinitorum (1748)* as a citation.

15. In the phrase *Lettres a une princesse d'Allemagne*, replace the one-letter word *a* with **à** (the character entity name is *agrave*). Mark the entire publication name as a citation.

16. In the third paragraph, mark the notation for *e* as a `var` element and replace *pi* with the character π (the character reference name is *pi*).

17. Enclose the next section of text from the line *The Most Beautiful Theorem?* up to (but not including) the line *Math High: A Site for Educators and Researchers* as an aside.

18. Mark the text *The Most Beautiful Theorem?* as an `h1` heading.

19. Mark the next five blocks of text as individual paragraphs.

20. In the first equation, mark the letters *e*, *i*, and *x* using the `var` element (but do not italicize the *i* in *sin*). Mark the term (ix) as a superscript.

21. In the second equation, replace *pi* with the character π. Mark the letters *e* and *i* using the `var` element. Mark (πi) as a superscript.

22. In the last paragraph, mark the notations for *e* and *i* with the `var` element and replace *pi* with π.

23. Mark the journal name *The Mathematical Intelligencer* as a citation.

24. Mark the final line in the file as a footer.

25. Save your changes to the file, and then verify that the page appears correctly in your Web browser.

26. Submit your completed files to your instructor, in either printed or electronic form, as requested.

Apply your knowledge of HTML to create a page showing text from a scene of a Shakespeare play.

APPLY

Case Problem 2

Data Files needed for the Case Problem: macbeth.jpg, macbethtxt.htm, macstyles.css, modernizr-1.5.js

Mansfield Classical Theatre   Steve Karls is the director of Mansfield Classical Theatre, a theatre company for young people located in Mansfield, Ohio. This summer the company is planning to perform the Shakespeare play *Macbeth*. Steve wants to put the text of the play on the company's Web site and has asked for your help in designing and completing the Web page. Steve wants a separate page for each scene from the play. A preview of the page you'll create for Act I, Scene 1 is shown in Figure 1-50. Steve has already typed the text of the scene. He needs you to supply the HTML code.

Figure 1-50 Macbeth Act I, Scene 1 Web page

Presented by: Mansfield Classical Theatre

ACT I

SCENE 1

Summary A thunderstorm approaches and three witches convene. They agree to confront the great Scot general Macbeth upon his victorious return from a war between Scotland and Norway. Soon, heroic Macbeth will receive the title of Thane of Cawdor from King Duncan. However, Macbeth learns from the witches that he is fated for greater things and he will be led down the path of destruction by his unquenchable ambition.

A desert place.

Thunder and lightning. Enter three Witches.

First Witch
> When shall we three meet again
> In thunder, lightning, or in rain?

Second Witch
> When the hurlyburly's done,
> When the battle's lost and won.

Third Witch
> That will be ere the set of sun.

First Witch
> Where the place?

Second Witch
> Upon the heath.

Third Witch
> There to meet with Macbeth.

First Witch
> I come, Graymalkin!

Second Witch
> Paddock calls.

Third Witch
> Anon.

ALL
> Fair is foul, and foul is fair:
> Hover through the fog and filthy air.

Exeunt

Go to Scene 2 ⇒

TEXT PROVIDED BY ONLINE SHAKESPEARE

Complete the following:

1. Open the **macbethtxt.htm** file from the tutorial.01\case2 folder included with your Data Files. Save the file as **macbeth.htm** in the same folder.

2. Enclose the entire Macbeth text within the structure of an HTML document including the `html`, `head`, and `body` elements. Add a doctype to the document head to indicate that the page is written in HTML5.

3. Within the head section, insert a comment containing the following text:

   Macbeth: Act I, Scene 1

   Author: *your name*

   Date: *the date*

4. Add the page title **Macbeth: Act I, Scene 1**.

5. Link the file to the **modernizr-1.5.js** script file and to the **macstyles.css** style sheet. Set the character set to **UTF-8**.

6. Within the `body` element, insert a heading group consisting of an `h1` heading and an `h2` heading. Within the `h1` heading, insert an inline image containing the *macbeth. jpg* image file. Specify **Macbeth** as the alternate text. Within the `h2` heading, enter the text **Presented by: Mansfield Classical Theatre**.

7. Enclose the text of the play within a `section` element.

8. Mark the text *ACT I* as an `h2` heading. Mark *SCENE 1* as an `h3` heading. Group the two headings within an `hgroup` element.

9. Mark the summary of the scene as a paragraph. Mark the word *Summary* using the strong element.

10. In the text of the play, mark the descriptions of setting, scene, and exits as separate paragraphs and italicize the text using the `i` element, as shown in Figure 1-50.

⊕ **EXPLORE** 11. Mark the dialog as a description list, with each character's name marked as a description term and each speech marked as a description. When a speech includes two lines, add a line break at the end of the first line to keep the speech on separate lines, as shown in the figure.

⊕ **EXPLORE** 12. Directly below the paragraph containing the text *Exeunt,* insert the line **Go to Scene 2**. Mark this line as a `div` element with the id value *direction*. At the end of this line, insert a **right arrow character** using the 8658 character number. Add horizontal rules directly above and below this statement.

13. Mark the line *Text provided by Online Shakespeare* as a footer. Make sure the `footer` element is below the `section` element.

14. Save your changes to the file, and then confirm the layout and content of the page in your Web browser.

15. Submit the completed files to your instructor, in either printed or electronic form, as requested.

Explore how to use HTML to create a recipe page.

CHALLENGE

Case Problem 3

Data Files needed for the Case Problem: dessertstyles.css, dessertweb.jpg, modernizr-1.5.js, torte.jpg, tortetxt.htm

dessertWEB   Amy Wu wants to take her enjoyment of cooking and her love of sharing recipes to the World Wide Web. She's interested in creating a new Web site called *dessertWEB* where other cooks can submit and review dessert recipes. Each page within her site will contain a photo and description of a dessert, along with a list of ingredients, cooking directions, and a list of reviews. Each recipe will be rated on a five-star scale. She already has information on one recipe: Apple Bavarian Torte. She's asked for your help in creating a Web page from the data she's collected. A preview of the completed page is shown in Figure 1-51.

Figure 1-51   dessertWeb menu page

dessertWEB

Apple Bavarian Torte (★★★★)

A classic European torte baked in a springform pan. Cream cheese, sliced almonds, and apples make this the perfect holiday treat (12 servings).

INGREDIENTS
- ½ cup butter
- ⅓ cup white sugar
- ¼ teaspoon vanilla extract
- 1 cup all-purpose flour
- 1 (8 ounce) package cream cheese
- ¼ cup white sugar
- 1 egg
- ½ teaspoon vanilla extract
- 6 apples - peeled, cored, and sliced
- ⅓ cup white sugar
- ½ teaspoon ground cinnamon
- ¼ cup sliced almonds

DIRECTIONS
1. Preheat oven to 450° F (230° C).
2. Cream together butter, sugar, vanilla, and flour.
3. Press crust mixture into the flat bottom of a 9-inch springform pan. Set aside.
4. In a medium bowl, blend cream cheese and sugar. Beat in egg and vanilla. Pour cheese mixture over crust.
5. Toss apples with sugar and cinnamon. Spread apple mixture over all.
6. Bake for 10 minutes. Reduce heat to 400° F (200° C) and continue baking for 25 minutes.
7. Sprinkle almonds over top of torte. Continue baking until lightly browned. Cool before removing from pan.

REVIEWS

★★★★
I loved the buttery taste of the crust which complements the apples very nicely.
— Reviewed on Sep. 22, 2014 *by MMASON.*

★★
Nothing special. I like the crust, but there was a little too much of it for my taste, and I liked the filling but there was too little of it. I thought the crunchy apples combined with the sliced almonds detracted from the overall flavor.
— Reviewed on Sep. 1, 2014 *by GLENDACHEF.*

★★★★★
Delicious!! I recommend microwaving the apples for 3 minutes before baking, to soften them. Great dessert - I'll be making it again for the holidays.
— Reviewed on August 28, 2014 *by BBABS.*

Complete the following:

1. Open the **tortetxt.htm** file from the tutorial.01\case3 folder included with your Data Files. Save the file as **torte.htm** in the same folder.
2. Add the structure of an HTML5 document around the recipe text. Within the `head` element, insert a comment containing the following text:
   Apple Bavarian Torte
   Author: *your name*
   Date: *the date*
3. Set the character set of the document to **ISO-8859-1**.
4. Link the document to the **modernizr-1.5.js** script file and the **dessertstyles.css** style sheet file.
5. Specify **Apple Bavarian Torte Recipe** as the page title.
6. Within the `body` element, add a `header` element. Within the `header` element, insert an `h1` heading containing the inline image **dessertweb.jpg** with the alternate text **dessertWEB**.

7. Enclose the recipe description, ingredients list, and directions within a `section` element. Enclose the recipe reviews within an `aside` element.

8. Mark the text *Apple Bavarian Torte* as an `h1` heading.

⊕ **EXPLORE**   9. Replace the text *(4 stars)* in the `h1` heading with a set of four **star symbols** (character number 9733).

⊕ **EXPLORE**   10. Directly below the `h1` heading, insert the inline image **torte.jpg**. Specify the alternate text **Torte image**. Set the width of the image to **250** pixels.

11. Mark the description of the dessert as a paragraph.

12. Mark *INGREDIENTS* and *DIRECTIONS* as `h2` headings.

13. Mark the list of ingredients as an unordered list. Mark the list of directions as an ordered list.

⊕ **EXPLORE**   14. Within the ingredients, replace the occurrences of 1/2 with the character symbol ½ (reference number 189), the occurrences of 1/4 with the symbol ¼ (reference number 188), and the occurrences of 1/3 with the symbol ⅓ (reference number 8531.)

⊕ **EXPLORE**   15. Replace each occurrence of the word *degrees* in the directions with the degree symbol (°) (character name *deg*).

16. Mark *REVIEWS* within the `aside` element as an `h1` heading.

17. Change the text of each customer star rating to a set of **star symbols** using character number 9733 placed within a paragraph.

⊕ **EXPLORE**   18. Enclose the text of each customer review in a paragraph nested within a `blockquote` element. Place the name of the reviewer and the date on a new line within that paragraph. Insert an **em-dash** (character name *mdash*) before the word *Reviewed* in each of the reviews. Enclose the date of each review within a `time` element and enclose by *reviewer* within a `cite` element where *reviewer* is the name of the reviewer.

19. Save your changes to the file, and then verify the layout and content of the page in your Web browser.

20. Submit the completed files to your instructor, in either printed or electronic form, as requested.

Test your knowledge of HTML and use your creativity to design a Web page for an exercise equipment company.

RESEARCH

Case Problem 4

Data Files needed for the Case Problem: logo.jpg, smith.jpg, and smith.txt

Body Systems   Body Systems is a leading manufacturer of home gyms. The company recently hired you to assist in developing its Web site. Your first task is to create a Web page for the LSM400, a popular weight machine sold by the company. You've been given a text file describing the features of the LSM400. You've also received two image files: one of the company's logo and one of the LSM400. You are free to supplement these files with any other resources available to you. You are responsible for the page's content and appearance.

Complete the following:

1. Create a new HTML5 file named **smith.htm** and save it in the tutorial.01\case4 folder included with your Data Files.

2. Add the appropriate doctype for HTML5 to the beginning of the file.

3. Add a comment to the document head describing the document's content and containing your name and the date.

4. Add an appropriate page title to the document head.

5. Set the character set of the file to **UTF-8**.

6. Use the contents of the **smith.txt** document (located in the tutorial.01\case4 folder) as the basis of the document body. Include at least one example of each of the following:
   - structural elements such as the `header`, `footer`, `section`, and `aside` elements
   - grouping elements including a heading and a paragraph
   - an ordered or unordered list
   - a text-level element
   - an inline image
   - a character entity reference or a character encoding number
7. Structure your HTML5 code so that it's easy for others to read and understand.
8. Save your changes to the file, and then open it in your Web browser to verify that it is readable.
9. Submit your completed files to your instructor, in either printed or electronic form, as requested.

ENDING SOLUTION FILES

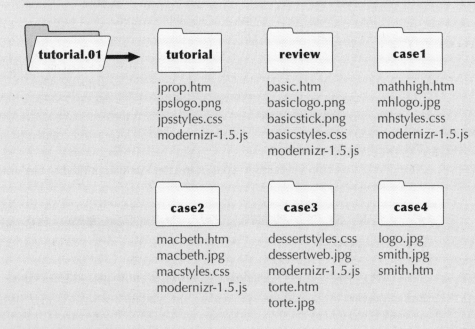

tutorial.01 → **tutorial**

jprop.htm
jpslogo.png
jpsstyles.css
modernizr-1.5.js

review

basic.htm
basiclogo.png
basicstick.png
basicstyles.css
modernizr-1.5.js

case1

mathhigh.htm
mhlogo.jpg
mhstyles.css
modernizr-1.5.js

case2

macbeth.htm
macbeth.jpg
macstyles.css
modernizr-1.5.js

case3

dessertstyles.css
dessertweb.jpg
modernizr-1.5.js
torte.htm
torte.jpg

case4

logo.jpg
smith.jpg
smith.htm

TUTORIAL **2**

OBJECTIVES

Session 2.1
- Explore how to storyboard a Web site
- Create navigation lists
- Create links between documents in a Web site
- Understand absolute and relative folder paths
- Set a base path
- Mark a location with the id attribute
- Create a link to an id

Session 2.2
- Mark an image as a link
- Create an image map
- Understand URLs
- Link to a resource on the Web
- Link to an e-mail address
- Work with hypertext attributes
- Work with metadata

Developing a Web Site

Creating a Web Site for Amateur Photographers

Case | *CAMshots*

Gerry Hayward is an amateur photographer and digital camera enthusiast. He's creating a Web site named *CAMshots*, where he can offer advice and information to people who are just getting started with digital photography, or who are long-time hobbyists like himself and are looking to share tips and ideas. Gerry's Web site will contain several pages, with each page dedicated to a particular topic. He has created a few sample pages for the Web site, but he hasn't linked them together. He has asked for your help in designing his site and creating links between the pages.

STARTING DATA FILES

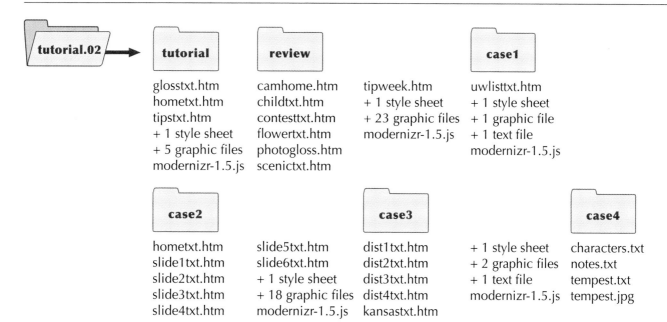

tutorial.02 →

tutorial
glosstxt.htm
hometxt.htm
tipstxt.htm
+ 1 style sheet
+ 5 graphic files
modernizr-1.5.js

review
camhome.htm
childtxt.htm
contesttxt.htm
flowertxt.htm
photogloss.htm
scenictxt.htm

tipweek.htm
+ 1 style sheet
+ 23 graphic files
modernizr-1.5.js

case1
uwlisttxt.htm
+ 1 style sheet
+ 1 graphic file
+ 1 text file
modernizr-1.5.js

case2
hometxt.htm
slide1txt.htm
slide2txt.htm
slide3txt.htm
slide4txt.htm

slide5txt.htm
slide6txt.htm
+ 1 style sheet
+ 18 graphic files
modernizr-1.5.js

case3
dist1txt.htm
dist2txt.htm
dist3txt.htm
dist4txt.htm
kansastxt.htm

+ 1 style sheet
+ 2 graphic files
+ 1 text file
modernizr-1.5.js

case4
characters.txt
notes.txt
tempest.txt
tempest.jpg

SESSION 2.1 VISUAL OVERVIEW

The nav element marks a list of hypertext links used to navigate through the pages in the Web site.

```
<nav>
    <ul>
        <li><a href="home.htm">Home</a></li>
        <li><a href="tips.htm">Tips</a></li>
        <li><a href="glossary.htm"> Glossary</a></li>
    </ul>
</nav>
```

The **<a> tag** is used to mark hyperlinks to external documents or to locations within the current document. The **href** attribute indicates the reference or address of the linked resource.

CAMshots

Tips   Photo G

| Home | Tips | Glossary |

Welcome to CAMshots, a site for people passion about digital photography. This site has grown d decades of photographic experience. I offer adv for both beginners and advanced users. I hope enjoy what you find, but please be considerate work it took to do all this. The entire site conten including all images and articles are copyrighted Please honor my work and do not copy anything without permission. If you are interested in publishing any of my images or articles or using in other ways, please contact me and we can di your needs. Happy Shooting!

— Gerry

By default, browsers underline hypertext links.

CAMSHOTS >>> ADVICE AND NEWS FROM THE

```
<a href="glossary.htm#flash_mode">Flash Mode</a>
```

Links to locations within a document are referenced using the form *file#id*, where file is the name of the file and id is the id marking the location within the file.

CREATING HYPERLINKS

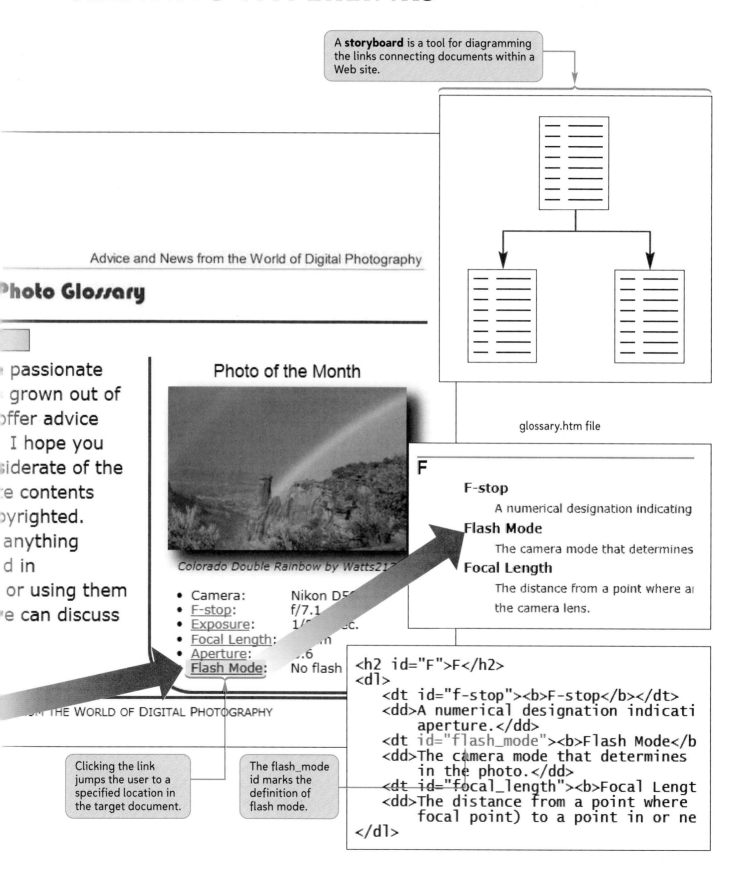

A **storyboard** is a tool for diagramming the links connecting documents within a Web site.

Advice and News from the World of Digital Photography

Photo Glossary

passionate
grown out of
offer **advice**
I hope you
siderate of the
e contents
pyrighted.
anything
d in
or using them
e can discuss

Photo of the Month

Colorado Double Rainbow by Watts21?

- Camera: Nikon D5
- F-stop: f/7.1
- Exposure: 1/   ec.
- Focal Length:
- Aperture: .6
- Flash Mode: No flash

THE WORLD OF DIGITAL PHOTOGRAPHY

glossary.htm file

F

F-stop
   A numerical designation indicating

Flash Mode
   The camera mode that determines

Focal Length
   The distance from a point where ar
   the camera lens.

```
<h2 id="F">F</h2>
<dl>
   <dt id="f-stop"><b>F-stop</b></dt>
   <dd>A numerical designation indicati
      aperture.</dd>
   <dt id="flash_mode"><b>Flash Mode</b
   <dd>The camera mode that determines
      in the photo.</dd>
   <dt id="focal_length"><b>Focal Lengt
   <dd>The distance from a point where
      focal point) to a point in or ne
</dl>
```

Clicking the link jumps the user to a specified location in the target document.

The flash_mode id marks the definition of flash mode.

Exploring Web Site Structures

You meet with Gerry to discuss his plans for the CAMshots Web site. Gerry has already created a prototype for the Web site containing three pages written in HTML5: One page is the site's home page and contains general information about CAMshots; the second page contains tips about digital photography; and the third page contains a partial glossary of photographic terms. The pages are not complete, nor are they linked to one another. You'll begin your work for Gerry by viewing these files in your text editor and browser.

To view Gerry's Web pages:

1. Start your text editor, and then open the **hometxt.htm**, **tipstxt.htm**, and **glosstxt.htm** files, located in the tutorial.02\tutorial folder included with your Data Files.

2. Within each file, go to the comment section at the top of the file and add **your name** and **the date** in the space provided.

3. Save the files as **home.htm**, **tips.htm**, and **glossary.htm**, respectively, in the tutorial.02\tutorial folder.

4. Take some time to review the HTML code within each document so that you understand the structure and content of the files.

5. Start your Web browser and open the **home.htm**, **tips.htm**, and **glossary.htm** files. Figure 2-1 shows the current layout and appearance of Gerry's three Web pages.

| Figure 2-1 | Versions of HTML |

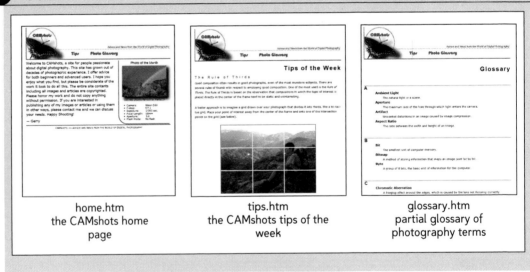

home.htm
the CAMshots home page

tips.htm
the CAMshots tips of the week

glossary.htm
partial glossary of photography terms

Gerry wants to create links among the three pages so that users can easily navigate from one page to another. Before you write code for the links, it's worthwhile to use a technique known as storyboarding to map out exactly how you want the pages to relate to each other. A storyboard is a diagram of a Web site's structure, showing all the pages in the site and indicating how they are linked together. Because Web sites use a variety of structures, it's important to storyboard your Web site before you start creating your pages. This helps you determine which structure works best for the type of information your site contains. A well-designed structure ensures that users will be able to navigate the site without getting lost or missing important information.

Every Web site should begin with a single **home page** that acts as a focal point for the Web site. It is usually the first page that users see. From that home page, you add links to other pages in the site, defining the site's overall structure. The Web sites you commonly encounter as you navigate the Web employ several different Web structures. You'll examine some of these structures to help you decide how to design your own sites.

Linear Structures

If you wanted to create an online version of a famous play, like Shakespeare's *Hamlet*, one method would be to link the individual scenes of the play in a long chain. Figure 2-2 shows the storyboard for this **linear structure**, in which each page is linked with the pages that follow and precede it. Readers navigate this structure by moving forward and backward through the pages, much as they might move forward and backward through the pages of a book.

Figure 2-2   **A linear structure**

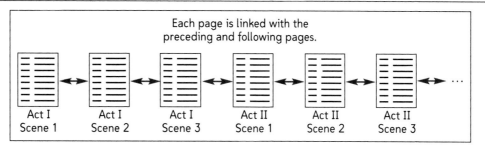

Linear structures work for Web sites that are small in size and have a clearly defined order of pages. However, they can be difficult to work with as the chain of pages increases in length. An additional problem is that in a linear structure, you move farther and farther away from the home page as you progress through the site. Because home pages often contain important general information about a site and its author, this is usually not the best design technique.

You can modify this structure to make it easier for users to return immediately to the home page or other main pages. Figure 2-3 shows this online play with an **augmented linear structure**, in which each page contains an additional link back to the opening page of each act.

Figure 2-3   **An augmented linear structure**

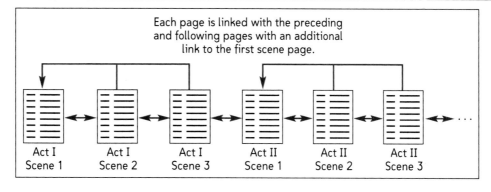

Hierarchical Structures

Another popular structure is the **hierarchical structure**, in which the home page links to pages dedicated to specific topics. Those pages, in turn, can be linked to even more specific topics. A hierarchical structure allows users to easily move from general to specific and back again. In the case of the online play, you could link an introductory page containing general information about the play to pages that describe each of the play's acts, and within each act you could include links to individual scenes. See Figure 2-4. Within this structure, a user could move quickly to a specific scene within the play, bypassing the need to move through each scene that precedes it.

Figure 2-4 **A hierarchical structure**

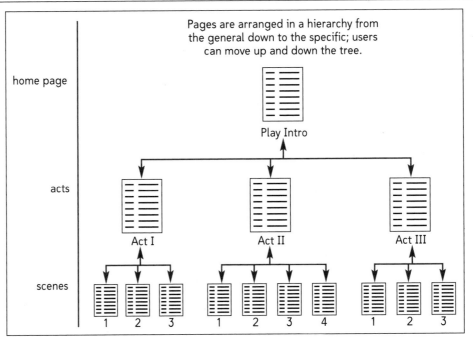

Pages are arranged in a hierarchy from the general down to the specific; users can move up and down the tree.

home page — Play Intro

acts — Act I, Act II, Act III

scenes — 1 2 3 | 1 2 3 4 | 1 2 3

Mixed Structures

With larger and more complex Web sites, you often need to use a combination of structures. Figure 2-5 shows the online play using a mixture of hierarchical and linear structures. The overall form is hierarchical, as users can move from a general introduction down to individual scenes; however, users can also move through the site in a linear fashion, going from act to act and scene to scene. Finally, each individual scene contains a link to the home page, allowing users to jump to the top of the hierarchy without moving through the different levels.

Figure 2-5   **A mixed structure**

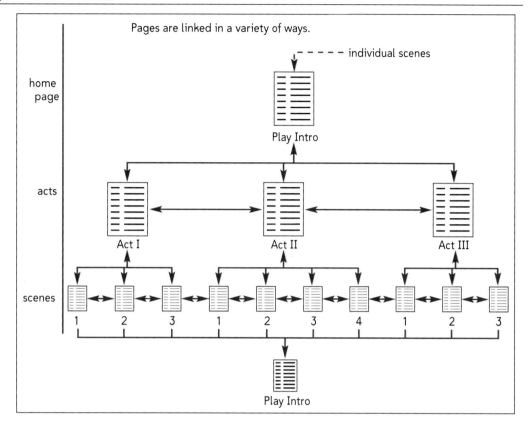

As these examples show, a little foresight can go a long way toward making your Web site easier to use. Also keep in mind that search results from a Web search engine such as Google or Yahoo! can point users to any page in your Web site—not just your home page—so they will need to be able to quickly understand what your site contains and how to navigate it. At a minimum, each page should contain a link to the site's home page or to the relevant main topic page. In some cases, you might want to supply your users with a **site index**, which is a page containing an outline of the entire site and its contents. Unstructured Web sites can be difficult and frustrating to use. Consider the storyboard of the site displayed in Figure 2-6.

Figure 2-6   **Web site with no coherent structure**

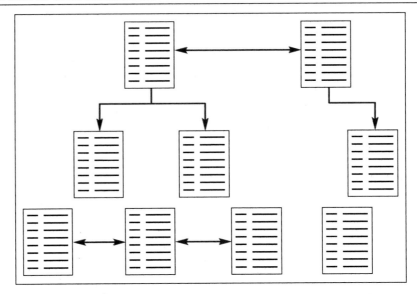

This confusing structure makes it difficult for users to grasp the site's contents and scope. The user might not even be aware of the presence of some pages because there are no connecting links, and some of the links point in only one direction. The Web is a competitive place; studies have shown that users who don't see how to get what they want within the first few seconds often leave a Web site. How long would a user spend on a site like the one shown in Figure 2-6?

Protected Structures

Sections of most commercial Web sites are off-limits except to subscribers and registered customers. As shown in Figure 2-7, these sites have a password-protected Web page that users must go through to get to the off-limits areas. The same Web site design principles apply to the protected section as the regular, open section of the site.

Figure 2-7   **A protected structure**

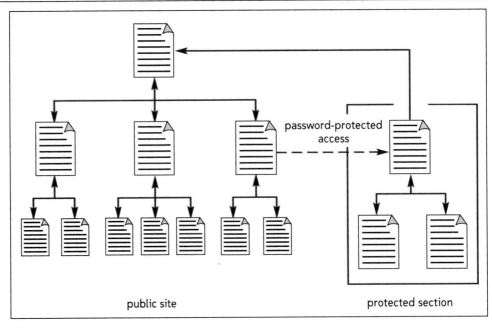

Storyboarding a protected structure is particularly important to ensure that no unauthorized access to the protected area is allowed in the site design.

Creating a Navigation List

Every Web site should include a **navigation list**, which is a list containing links to the main topic areas of the site. Ideally, this same list should appear prominently on every page, usually near the top of the page as part of the header or as a sidebar to the main content.

HTML5 introduced the `nav` structural element to make it easier to mark up navigation lists. The syntax of the element is

```
<nav>
    list of navigation links
</nav>
```

where *list of navigation links* is a list of elements that are linked to other pages on the Web site. Prior to HTML5, such lists would often be inserted within the generic `div` element as

```
<div id="id">
    list of navigation links
</div>
```

where *id* is whatever id the page author would supply to identify the navigation list.

Gerry suggests you add the topics for his three sample pages as an unordered list within the `nav` element as follows:

```
<nav>
    <ul>
        <li>Home</li>
        <li>Tips</li>
        <li>Glossary</li>
    </ul>
</nav>
```

Gerry has already designed styles for these new elements and placed them within the camstyles.css style sheet. The style sheet will format the elements so that the list appears as a horizontally aligned set of boxes. As Gerry adds more sample pages, he can easily extend this list to include the new topics, but for now he needs only these three.

Add this navigation list to each of the three sample pages that Gerry has given you.

To create the navigation list:

1. Return to the **home.htm** file in your text editor.

2. At the top of the file directly below the header element, insert the following code as shown in Figure 2-8:

```
<nav>
    <ul>
        <li>Home</li>
        <li>Tips</li>
        <li>Glossary</li>
    </ul>
</nav>
```

Figure 2-8 | **Marking a navigation list**

navigation list marked
with the nav element

```
<body>
    <header>
        <img src="camshots.jpg" alt="CAMshots" />
    </header>

    <nav>
        <ul>
            <li>Home</li>
            <li>Tips</li>
            <li>Glossary</li>
        </ul>
    </nav>
```

▶ **3.** Save your changes to the file.

▶ **4.** Go to the **tips.htm** file in your text editor and then repeat Steps 2 and 3, placing the navigation list in the same place as you did in the home.htm file and saving your changes.

▶ **5.** Go to the **glossary.htm** file in your text editor and then repeat Steps 2 and 3 to add a navigation list to that file.

▶ **6.** Open or refresh the **home.htm** file in your Web browser. Verify that the navigation list appears directly below the page header as shown in Figure 2-9.

Figure 2-9 | **Navigation list in the CAMshots home page**

navigation list
formatted as a
horizontal set
of boxes

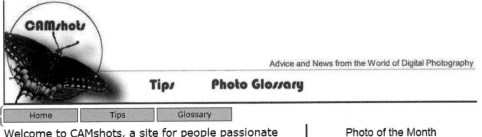

Welcome to CAMshots, a site for people passionate about digital photography. This site has grown out of decades of photographic experience. I offer advice for both beginners and advanced users. I hope you enjoy what you find, but please be considerate of the work it took to do all this. The entire site contents including all images and articles are copyrighted. Please honor my work and do not copy anything without permission. If you are interested in publishing any of my images or articles or using them in other ways, please contact me and we can discuss your needs. Happy Shooting!

— Gerry

Photo of the Month

Colorado Double Rainbow by Watts213

- Camera: Nikon D50
- F-stop: f/7.1
- Exposure: 1/200 sec.
- Focal Length: 18mm
- Aperture: 3.6
- Flash Mode: No flash

CAMSHOTS >>> ADVICE AND NEWS FROM THE WORLD OF DIGITAL PHOTOGRAPHY

▶ **7.** Open or refresh the **tips.htm** and **glossary.htm** files in your Web browser and verify that a similar navigation list appears at the top of those pages.

Navigation Lists and Web Accessibility

One challenge of Web design is creating Web documents that are accessible to users with disabilities. Studies indicate that about 20% of the population has some type of disability. Many of these disabilities don't affect users' capacity to interact with the Web. But in some cases, users may need specialized Web browsers, such as screen readers that provide Web content aurally for visually impaired users.

To accommodate these users, Web page authors can take advantage of the structural elements provided by HTML5. For example, the nav element can allow users to either quickly jump to a list of links or bypass such a list if they are more interested in the content of the current document. Prior to HTML5 and the nav element, there was no way of differentiating one list from another, and thus disabled users would be forced to wait through a rendering of the same navigation list for each page they visited.

Because support for HTML5 is still in its infancy at the time of this writing, most specialized browsers have not incorporated features that enable users to quickly access the structural elements of most interest to them. However, as the specifications for HTML5 are finalized and fully supported by the browser market, this ability will become more commonly supported. Thus you should use the nav element and other structural elements from HTML5 to provide more information to browsers about the content and structure of your Web documents.

Working with Hypertext Links

Now that you've added a navigation list to each of the three sample pages, you will change each item in those lists into a hypertext link so that users can easily move between the three sample pages. Figure 2-10 shows the storyboard for the simple structure you have in mind.

Figure 2-10   **Storyboard for the CAMshots sample Web site**

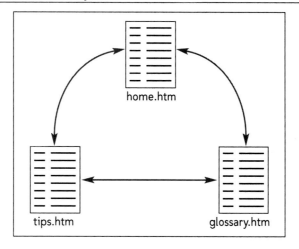

Hypertext links are created by enclosing some document content within a set of opening and closing <a> tags. The general syntax to create a hypertext link is

```
<a href="reference">content</a>
```

where *reference* is the location being linked to and *content* is the document content that is being marked as a link. The *reference* value can be a page on the World Wide

Web, a local file, an e-mail address, or a network server. For example, to create a hypertext link to the tips.htm file, you could enter the following code:

```
<a href="tips.htm">Photography Tips</a>
```

This code marks the text *Photography Tips* as a hypertext link. If a user clicks the text, the browser will load the linked resource (tips.htm). Note that filenames are case sensitive on some operating systems, such as the UNIX operating system. Web servers running on those systems differentiate between files named tips.htm and Tips.htm. For this reason, you might find that links you create on your computer do not work when you transfer your files to a Web server. To avoid this problem, the current standard is to always use lowercase filenames for all Web site files and to avoid using special characters and blank spaces.

Most browsers underline hypertext links unless a different style is specified in a user-defined style sheet. The font color of a link also changes based on whether or not the user has also visited the linked resource. By default, most browsers display hypertext links as follows:

- An unvisited link is underlined and blue.
- A previously visited link is underlined and purple.
- A link currently being clicked or activated is underlined and red.

However, Web page authors can use CSS to override these default settings.

TIP

Keep your filenames short and descriptive so that users are less apt to make a typing error when accessing your Web site.

REFERENCE

Marking a Hypertext Link

- To mark content as a hypertext link, use

```
<a href="reference">content</a>
```

where *reference* is the location being linked to and *content* is the document content that is being marked as a link.

You'll mark the names of the three sample pages in the navigation list you just created as hypertext links.

To create a hypertext link to a document:

1. Return to the **home.htm** file in your text editor and go to the navigation list at the top of the page.

2. Mark the text *Home* as a hypertext link using a set of <a> tags as follows:

```
<a href="home.htm">Home</a>
```

3. Mark the text *Tips* as a hypertext link using the following code:

```
<a href="tips.htm">Tips</a>
```

4. Mark the text *Glossary* as a hypertext link as follows:

```
<a href="glossary.htm">Glossary</a>
```

Figure 2-11 highlights the revised text in the home.htm file.

Figure 2-11   **Marking hypertext links in the navigation list**

reference of the
hypertext link

```
<nav>
    <ul>
        <li><a href="home.htm">Home</a></li>
        <li><a href="tips.htm">Tips</a></li>
        <li><a href="glossary.htm">Glossary</a></li>
    </ul>
</nav>
```

5. Save your changes to the file.

6. Go to the **tips.htm** file in your text editor and then repeat Steps 2 through 5 to change the text of the navigation list to hypertext links, saving your changes.

7. Go to the **glossary.htm** file in your text editor and then repeat Steps 2 through 5, saving your changes.

Now that you've added hypertext links to each of the three documents, you'll test those links in your browser.

8. Reload or refresh the **home.htm** file in your Web browser. As shown in Figure 2-12, the entries in the navigation list are underlined, providing a visual clue to the user that they are hypertext links.

Figure 2-12   **Viewing hypertext links in the navigation list**

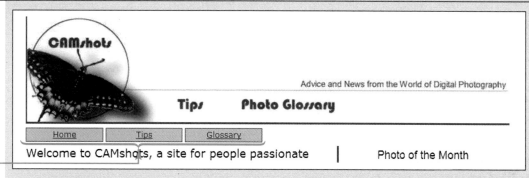

hypertext links
underlined by default

9. Click the **Tips** link in the navigation list. The Tips page should open in your browser.

10. Within the Tips page, click the **Glossary** link in the navigation list and then verify that the Glossary page opens.

11. Within the Glossary page, click the **Home** link in the navigation list to return to the CAMshots home page.

Trouble? If the links do not work, check the spelling of the filenames in the `href` attributes of the `<a>` tags. Because some Web servers require you to match capitalization in a filename, you should verify this in your attributes as well.

INSIGHT

Interpreting the <a> Tag in Different Versions of HTML

The <a> tag is treated slightly differently in versions of HTML prior to HTML5. In HTML 4.01 and XHTML, the <a> tag can be used to enclose only text-level elements and should not be used to group content or structural elements. This means that the code

```
<a href="home.htm">
   <p>Go to the home page</p>
</a>
```

would not be allowed because the hyperlink is applied to an entire paragraph. HTML5 does not make this distinction, allowing the <a> tag to enclose text-level, grouping, and structural elements.

A second important difference is that in HTML 4.01 and XHTML, the <a> tag can also be used as an anchor to mark specific locations within the document. For that reason, the <a> tag is commonly referred to as the tag for the anchor element. HTML5 does not support this interpretation; the <a> tag can be used only to mark hypertext links.

Attributes of the a Element

The a element supports several attributes in addition to the href attribute. Some of these attributes are listed in Figure 2-13.

Figure 2-13 **Attributes of the anchor (a) element**

Attribute	Description
charset="*encoding*"	Specifies the character encoding used in the linked resource (*not supported in HTML5*)
href="*url*"	Indicates the resource targeted by the hypertext link
media="*media type*"	Indicates the media device in which the linked resource should be viewed (*HTML5*)
name="*name*"	Assigns a name for the section anchored by the <a> tag (*not supported in HTML5*)
rel="*relationship*"	Specifies the relationship between the current document and the linked resource
ping="*url*"	A space-separated list of resources that get notified when the user follows the hyperlink (*HTML5*)
target="*target_type*"	Specifies where to open the linked resource
type="*mime-type*"	Specifies the content (the mime-type) of the linked resource

For example, the following code uses the `media` attribute to indicate to browsers that the linked resource is suitable for printing:

```
<a href="orderform.htm" media="print">
   View an Order Form
</a>
```

The `media` attribute doesn't instruct the browser to print the linked file; it just tells the browser for what kind of output media the file has been designed. On the other hand, the following code uses the `type` attribute to indicate the file format of the linked file:

```
<a href="photo.png" mime-type="image/png">
   View the photo of the month
</a>
```

In this case, the browser is forewarned that the linked file is a graphic image file in the PNG format. Some browsers can use the `mime-type` attribute to load applications and programs to view the linked document. But in most cases, the browser determines the file format as it receives the document from the Web server, and thus no `mime-type` attribute is required.

Specifying a Folder Path

In the links you just created, you specified the filename but not the location of the file. When you specify only the filename, the browser assumes that the file is in the same folder as the document containing the hypertext link. However, large Web sites containing hundreds of documents often place documents in separate folders to make them easier to manage.

As Gerry adds more files to his Web site, he will probably want to use folders to organize the files. Figure 2-14 shows a preview of how Gerry might employ those folders. In this case, the top folder containing all of the content of the Web site is named *camshots*. Gerry might place some of his HTML files within the *pages* folder, which he would then divide into three subfolders, named *tips*, *glossary*, and *articles*. He could also create separate folders for the images and video clips used on his Web site.

Figure 2-14 A sample folder structure

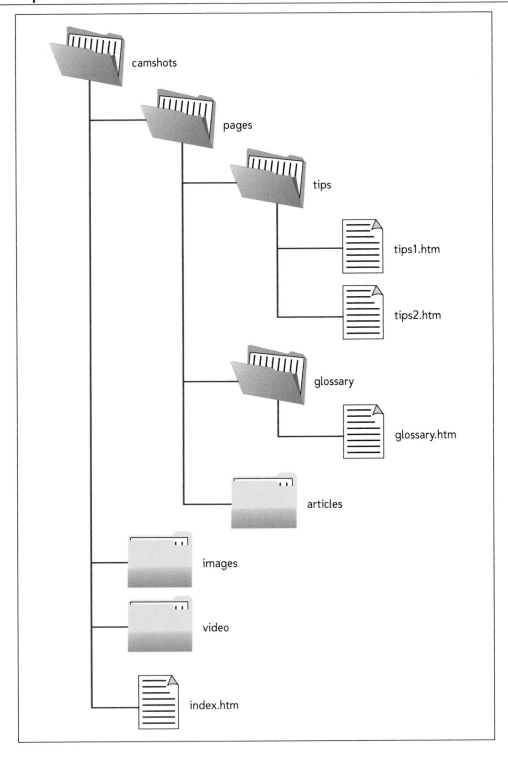

To create a link to a file located in a folder other than the current document's folder, you must specify that file's location, or **path**. HTML supports two kinds of paths: absolute and relative.

Absolute Paths

An **absolute path** specifies a file's precise location within the entire folder structure of a computer. Absolute paths employ the syntax

```
/folder1/folder2/folder3/file
```

where *folder1* is the top folder in the hierarchy, followed by *folder2*, *folder3*, and so forth, down to the file you want to link to. Figure 2-15 shows how you would express absolute paths to the four files listed in Figure 2-14.

Figure 2-15	Absolute paths

Absolute Path	Interpretation
/camshots/pages/tips/tips1.htm	The tips1.htm file located in the pages/tips subfolder
/camshots/pages/tips/tips2.htm	The tips2.htm file located in the pages/tips subfolder
/camshots/pages/glossary/glossary.htm	The glossary.htm file located in the pages/glossary subfolder
/camshots/index.htm	The index.htm file located in the camshots folder

If files are located on different drives as well as in different folders, you must include the drive letter in the path

```
/drive|/folder1/folder2/folder3/file
```

where *drive* is the letter assigned to the drive. For example, the tips1.htm file located on drive C in the */camshots/pages/tips* folder would have the absolute path

```
/C|/camshots/pages/tips/tips1.htm
```

Note that you don't have to include a drive letter if the linked document is located on the same drive as the current file.

Relative Paths

When many folders and subfolders are involved, absolute paths can be cumbersome and confusing to use. For this reason, most Web designers prefer to use relative paths. A **relative path** specifies a file's location in relation to the location of the current document. If the file is in the same location as the current document, the relative path is simply the filename. If the file is in a subfolder of the current document, include the name of the subfolder without the forward slash, as follows

```
folder/file
```

where *folder* is the name of the subfolder, which is also known as a **child folder**. Note that folders used in relative paths are often referenced using relative names, such as parent, child, sibling, and so forth. For example, to go farther down the folder tree to other sub-folders, include those folder names in the relative path separated by forward slashes, as in

```
folder1/folder2/folder3/file
```

where *folder1*, *folder2*, *folder3*, and so forth are subfolders, or **descendent folders**, of the current folder. Going in the opposite direction, a relative path moving up the folder tree to a **parent folder** is indicated by starting the path with a double period (..) followed by a forward slash and the name of the file. Thus, the relative path

```
../file
```

references the *file* document located in the parent folder. Finally, to reference a different folder on the same level as the current folder, known as a **sibling folder**, you move up the folder tree using the double period (..) to the parent and then back down to a different folder. The general syntax is

```
../folder/file
```

where *folder* is the name of the sibling folder. Figure 2-16 shows the relative paths to the six files in the tree from Figure 2-14, starting from the *camshots/pages/tips* subfolder.

Figure 2-16   Relative paths

Relative Path from the /camshots/pages/tips Subfolder	Interpretation
tips1.htm	The tips1.htm file located in the current folder
tips2.htm	The tips2.htm file located in the current folder
../glossary/glossary.htm	The glossary.htm file located in the sibling glossary folder
../../index.htm	The index.htm file located in the parent camshots folder

You should almost always use relative paths in your links. If you have to move your files to a different computer or server, you can move the entire folder structure without having to edit the relative paths you've created. If you use absolute paths, you will probably have to revise each link to reflect the new location of the folder tree on the computer.

Setting the Base Path

As you've just seen, a browser resolves relative paths based on the location of the current document. You can change this behavior by using the base element to specify a different starting location for all relative paths. The base element has the syntax

```
<base href="path" />
```

where *path* is the folder location that you want the browser to use when resolving relative paths in the current document. The base element must be nested within the head element of the HTML file so it can be applied to all hypertext links found within the document.

The base element is useful when a single document is moved to a new folder. Rather than rewriting all of the relative paths to reflect the document's new location, the base element redirects browsers to the document's old location, allowing any relative paths to be resolved as they were before.

PROSKILLS

Problem Solving: Managing Your Web Site

Web sites can quickly grow from a couple of pages to dozens or hundreds of pages. As the size of a site increases, it becomes more difficult to get a clear picture of the site's structure and content. Imagine deleting or moving a file in a Web site that contains dozens of folders and hundreds of files. Could you easily project the effect of this change? Would all of your hypertext links still work after you moved or deleted the file?

To effectively manage a Web site, you should follow a few important rules. The first is to be consistent in how you structure the site. If you decide to collect all image files in one folder, you should continue that practice as you add more pages and images. Web sites are more likely to break down if files and folders are scattered throughout the server without a consistent rule or pattern. Decide on a structure early and stick with it.

The second rule is to create a folder structure that matches the structure of the Web site itself. If the pages can be easily categorized into different groups, those groupings should also be reflected in the groupings of the subfolders. The names you assign to your files and folders should also reflect their uses on the Web site. This makes it easier for you to predict how modifying a file or folder might impact other pages on the site.

Finally, you should document your work by adding comments to each new Web page. Comments are useful not only for colleagues who may be working on the site, but also for the author who must revisit those files months or even years after creating them. The comments should include:

- The page's filename and location
- The page's author and the date the page was initially created
- A list of any supporting files used in the document, such as image and audio files
- A list of the files that link to the page, and their locations
- A list of the files that the page links to, and their locations

By following these rules, you can reduce a lot of the headaches associated with maintaining a large and complicated Web site.

Linking to Locations within a Document

Gerry has studied the navigation lists you created and would like you to add another navigation list to the Glossary page. Recall that the Glossary page contains a list of digital photography terms. The page is very long, requiring users to scroll through the document to find a term of interest. Gerry would like you to create a navigation list containing the letters A through Z. From this list, Gerry wants to give users the ability to jump to a specific section in the glossary matching the clicked letter.

See Figure 2-17.

Figure 2-17 | **Jumping to a location within a document**

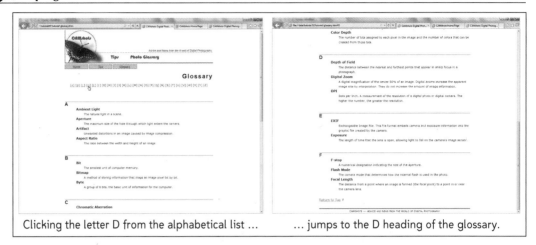

Clicking the letter D from the alphabetical list ...   ... jumps to the D heading of the glossary.

Add the navigation list to the glossary page now.

To create the navigation list:

1. Return to the **glossary.htm** file in your text editor.

2. Scroll down to the section element. Directly below the h1 *Glossary* heading, insert the following navigation list (see Figure 2-18):

```
<nav>
   [A] [B] [C]
   [D] [E] [F]
   [G] [H] [I]
   [J] [K] [L]
   [M] [N] [O]
   [P] [Q] [R]
   [S] [T] [U]
   [V] [W] [X]
   [Y] [Z]
</nav>
```

Figure 2-18 | **Adding a navigation element to the glossary**

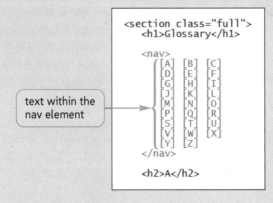

text within the nav element

3. Save your changes to the file.

Marking Locations with the `id` Attribute

To enable users to jump to a specific location within a document, you first need to mark that location. One way of doing this is to add the `id` attribute to an element at that location in the document. Recall that the syntax of the `id` attribute is

```
id="text"
```

where *text* is the name you want to assign to the id. For example, the following code marks an `h2` element with an id of `H`:

```
<h2 id="H">H</h2>
```

Note that id names must be unique. If you assign the same id name to more than one element on a Web page, browsers use the first occurrence of the id name. XHTML documents are rejected if they contain elements with duplicate ids. Id names are also case sensitive and most browsers other than Internet Explorer differentiate between ids named, for example, *top* and *TOP*.

REFERENCE

Defining an Element id

- To define the id of a specific element in a Web document, use the attribute

  ```
  id="text"
  ```

  where *text* is the value of the element id.

The Glossary page contains only a partial list of the photography terms that Gerry will eventually add to his Web site. For now, you'll mark only sections in the glossary corresponding to the letters A through F.

To add the `id` attribute to `h2` headings:

1. Scroll down the file and locate the `h2` heading for the letter A. Within the opening `<h2>` tag, insert the following attribute:

   ```
   id="A"
   ```

2. Locate the `h2` heading for the letter B and insert the following attribute in the opening `<h2>` tag:

   ```
   id="B"
   ```

   Figure 2-19 highlights the revised code.

Figure 2-19 | Adding the id attribute to h2 headings

h2 heading marked with an id value of "A"

h2 heading marked with an id value of "B"

```
<h2 id="A">A</h2>
<dl>
    <dt><b>Ambient Light</b></dt>
    <dd>The natural light in a scene.</dd>
    <dt><b>Aperture</b></dt>
    <dd>The maximum size of the hole through which light
        enters the camera.</dd>
    <dt><b>Artifact</b></dt>
    <dd>Unwanted distortions in an image caused by image
        compression.</dd>
    <dt><b>Aspect Ratio</b></dt>
    <dd>The ratio between the width and height of an
        image.</dd>
</dl>

<h2 id="B">B</h2>
<dl>
    <dt><b>Bit</b></dt>
    <dd>The smallest unit of computer memory.</dd>
    <dt><b>Bitmap</b></dt>
    <dd>A method of storing information that maps an image
        pixel bit by bit.</dd>
    <dt><b>Byte</b></dt>
    <dd>A group of 8 bits, the basic unit of information
        for the computer.</dd>
</dl>
```

3. Continue going down the file, adding id attributes to the opening <h2> heading tags for C, D, E, and F corresponding to the letters of those headings.

For longer documents like the Glossary page, it's also helpful for users to be able to jump directly from the bottom to the top of the page, rather than having to scroll back up. With that in mind, you'll also add an id attribute marking the element at the top of the page.

To mark the top of the page:

1. Scroll up the **glossary.htm** file in your text editor and locate the header element directly below the opening <body> tag.

2. Insert the following attribute within the opening <header> tag, as shown in Figure 2-20:

   id="top"

Figure 2-20 | Adding the id attribute to the page header

header marked with an id value of "top"

```
<body>
    <header id="top">
        <img src="camshots.jpg" alt="CAMshots" />
    </header>
```

3. Save your changes to the file.

Linking to an id

Once you've marked an element using the `id` attribute, you can create a hypertext link to that element using the a element

```
<a href="#id">content</a>
```

where *id* is the value of the `id` attribute of the element. For example, to create a link to the h2 heading for the letter A in the glossary document, you would enter the following code:

```
<a href="#A">A</a>
```

You'll change each entry on the Glossary page to a hypertext link pointing to the section of the glossary corresponding to the selected letter.

To change the list of letters to hypertext links:

1. Locate the letter A in the list of letters at the top of the **glossary.htm** file.

2. After the [character, insert the following opening tag:

   ```
   <a href="#A">
   ```

3. Between the letter A and the] character, insert the closing </a> tag. Figure 2-21 shows the revised code.

Figure 2-21	Marking a hypertext link for "A"

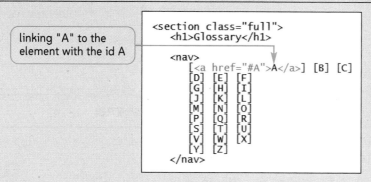

linking "A" to the element with the id A

```
<section class="full">
    <h1>Glossary</h1>

    <nav>
        [<a href="#A">A</a>] [B] [C]
        [D] [E] [F]
        [G] [H] [I]
        [J] [K] [L]
        [M] [N] [O]
        [P] [Q] [R]
        [S] [T] [U]
        [V] [W] [X]
        [Y] [Z]
    </nav>
```

Make sure you include the pound symbol (#) in the hypertext link, and ensure that the id text matches both upper- and lowercase letters in the linked id.

4. Mark the letters B through F in the list as hypertext links pointing to the appropriate h2 headings in the document. Figure 2-22 shows the revised code for the list of letters.

Figure 2-22	Hypertext links for the list of letters

```
<nav>
    [<a href="#A">A</a>] [<a href="#B">B</a>] [<a href="#C">C</a>]
    [<a href="#D">D</a>] [<a href="#E">E</a>] [<a href="#F">F</a>]
    [G] [H] [I]
    [J] [K] [L]
    [M] [N] [O]
    [P] [Q] [R]
    [S] [T] [U]
    [V] [W] [X]
    [Y] [Z]
</nav>
```

Gerry also wants you to create a hypertext link at the bottom of the file that points to the top. You'll use the `id` attribute you created in the last set of steps.

5. Scroll to the bottom of the file and locate the text *Return to Top*.

6. Mark the text as a hyperlink, pointing to the element with an id value of *top*. See Figure 2-23.

Figure 2-23   **Hypertext link to jump to the top**

link to the element
with the id *top*

```
    <div><a href="#top">Return to Top</a> &#8657;</div>
  </section>

  <footer>
      <address>
          CAMshots &#8250;&#8250;&#8250; Advice and News from
          the World of Digital Photography
      </address>
  </foooter>
```

---

7. Save your changes to the file and then reload or refresh the **glossary.htm** file in your Web browser. As shown in Figure 2-24, the letters A through F in the alphabetical list are displayed as hypertext links.

8. Click the link for **F** and verify that you jump down to the end of the document, where the photographic terms starting with the letter F are listed.

Figure 2-24   **Hypertext links in the glossary page**

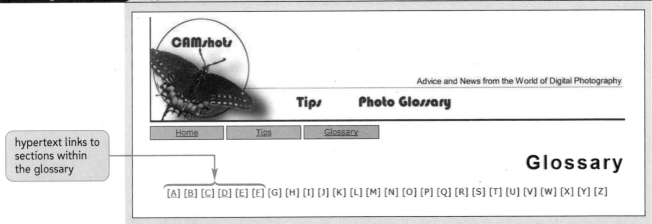

hypertext links to
sections within
the glossary

---

9. Click the **Return to Top** hypertext link and verify that you jump back to the top of the document.

10. Click the other links within the document and verify that you jump to the correct sections of the glossary.

Trouble? The browser cannot scroll farther than the end of the page. As a result, you might not see any difference between jumping to the E section of the glossary and jumping to the F section.

Anchors and the name *Attribute*

Early Web pages did not support the use of the id attribute as a way of marking locations within a document. Instead, they used the <a> tag as an **anchor** or bookmark using the name attribute

```
<a name="anchor">content</a>
```

where *anchor* is the name of the anchor that marks the location of the document content. For example, to add an anchor to an h2 heading, you would enter the following code:

```
<h2><a name="A">A</a></h2>
```

Marking a location with an anchor does not change your document's appearance in any way; it merely creates a destination within your document. You use the same syntax to link to locations marked with an anchor as you would with locations marked with id attributes. To link to the above anchor, you could use the following code:

```
<a href="#A">A</a>
```

The use of anchors is a deprecated feature of HTML and is not supported in strict applications of XHTML. The name attribute is not part of HTML5, but you will still see anchors used in older code and in code generated by HTML editors and converters.

Creating Links to ids in Other Documents

Gerry knows that the glossary will be one of the most useful parts of his Web site, especially for novice photographers. However, he's also aware that most people do not read through glossaries. He would like to create links from the words he uses in his articles to glossary entries so that readers of his articles can quickly access definitions for terms they don't understand. His articles are not on the same page as his Glossary page, so he'll have to create a link between those pages and specific glossary entries.

To create a link to a specific location within a document, mark the hypertext link as follows

```
<a href="reference#id">content</a>
```

where *reference* is a reference to an HTML or XHTML file and *id* is the id of an element marked with the *id* attribute within that file. For example, the HTML code

```
<a href="glossary.htm#D">"D" terms in the Glossary</a>
```

creates a hypertext link to the D entries in the glossary.htm file. Note that this assumes that the glossary.htm file is located in the same folder as the document containing the hypertext link. If not, you have to include either the absolute or relative path information along with the filename, as described earlier.

Linking to an id

- To link to a specific location within the current file, use

  `<a href="#id">content</a>`

  where *id* is the id value of an element within the document.
- To link to a specific location in another file, use

  `<a href="reference#id">content</a>`

  where *reference* is a reference to an external file and *id* is the id value of an element in that file.

On Gerry's home page, he wants to showcase a Photo of the Month, displaying a photo that his readers might find interesting or useful in their own work. Along with the photo, he has included the digital camera settings used in taking the photo. Many of the camera settings are described on the Glossary page. Gerry suggests that you create a link between the setting name and the glossary entry. The five entries he wants to link to are F-stop, Exposure, Focal Length, Aperture, and Flash Mode. Your first step is to mark these entries in the glossary using the id attribute.

To mark the glossary entries:

1. Return to the **glossary.htm** file in your text editor.

2. Scroll through the file and locate the *Aperture* definition term.

3. As shown in Figure 2-25, within the opening `<dt>` tag, insert the following attribute:

   `id="aperture"`

Figure 2-25   Adding the id attribute to the aperture definition

```
<h2 id="A">A</h2>
<dl>
    <dt><b>Ambient Light</b></dt>
    <dd>The natural light in a scene.</dd>
    <dt id="aperture"><b>Aperture</b></dt>
    <dd>The maximum size of the hole through which light
        enters the camera.</dd>
    <dt><b>Artifact</b></dt>
    <dd>Unwanted distortions in an image caused by image
        compression.</dd>
    <dt><b>Aspect Ratio</b></dt>
    <dd>The ratio between the width and height of an
        image.</dd>
</dl>
```

4. Scroll down the file and locate the *Exposure* definition term.

5. Within the opening `<dt>` tag, insert the following attribute:

   `id="exposure"`

6. Go to the F section of the glossary and mark the terms with the following ids (see Figure 2-26):

   F-stop with the id `f-stop`

   Flash Mode with the id `flash_mode`

   Focal Length with the id `focal_length`

| Figure 2-26 | Adding ids to the other photographic definitions |

```
<h2 id="E">E</h2>
<dl>
    <dt><b>EXIF</b></dt>
    <dd>Exchangeable Image File. This file format embeds camera
        and exposure information into the graphic file created
        by the camera.</dd>
    <dt id="exposure"><b>Exposure</b></dt>
    <dd>The length of time that the lens is open, allowing light
        to fall on the camera's image sensor.</dd>
</dl>

<h2 id="F">F</h2>
<dl>
    <dt id="f-stop"><b>F-stop</b></dt>
    <dd>A numerical designation indicating the size of the
        aperture.</dd>
    <dt id="flash_mode"><b>Flash Mode</b></dt>
    <dd>The camera mode that determines how the internal flash is used
        in the photo.</dd>
    <dt id="focal_length"><b>Focal Length</b></dt>
    <dd>The distance from a point where an image is formed (the
        focal point) to a point in or near the camera lens.</dd>
</dl>
```

 7. Save your changes to the **glossary.htm** file.

Next you'll go to the Home page and create links from these terms in the Photo of the Month description to their entries on the Glossary page.

To create links to the glossary entries:

 1. Open the **home.htm** file in your text editor.

 2. Scroll down the file and locate the *F-stop* term in the unordered list.

 3. Mark *F-stop* as a hypertext link using the following code:

   `<a href="glossary.htm#f-stop">F-stop</a>`

 4. Mark *Exposure* as a hypertext link using the following code:

   `<a href="glossary.htm#exposure">Exposure</a>`

 5. Mark the remaining three entries in the unordered list as hypertext pointing to their corresponding entries on the Glossary page. Figure 2-27 highlights the revised code in the file.

Figure 2-27   **Linking to a location within another document**

```
<aside>
   <h1>Photo of the Month</h1>

   <figure>
      <img src="rainbow.png" alt="Photo" />
      <figcaption>Colorado Double Rainbow by Watts213</i></figcaption>
   </figure>

   <ul>
      <li>Camera:
                 
         Nikon D50
      </li>
      <li><a href="glossary.htm#f-stop">F-stop</a>:
                  
         f/7.1
      </li>
      <li><a href="glossary.htm#exposure">Exposure</a>:
               
         1/200 sec.
      </li>
      <li><a href="glossary.htm#focal_length">Focal Length</a>:
          
         18mm
      </li>
      <li><a href="glossary.htm#aperture">Aperture</a>:
                
         3.6
      </li>
      <li><a href="glossary.htm#flash_mode">Flash Mode</a>:
            
         No flash
      </li>
   </ul>
</aside>
```

document   element id

6. Save your changes to the file.

7. Refresh the **home.htm** file in your Web browser. As shown in Figure 2-28, the settings from the Photo of the Month description are now displayed as hypertext links.

Figure 2-28   **Linked photography terms**

Photo of the Month

Colorado Double Rainbow by Watts213

- Camera: Nikon D50
- F-stop: f/7.1
- Exposure: 1/200 sec.
- Focal Length: 18mm
- Aperture: 3.6
- Flash Mode: No flash

hypertext links to the definitions in the glossary page

8. Click the **F-stop** hypertext link and verify that you jump to the Glossary page with the F-stop entry displayed in the browser window.

9. Return to the CAMshots home page and click the hypertext links for the other terms in the list of photo settings, verifying that you jump to the section of the glossary that displays each term's definition.

PROSKILLS

Written Communication: Creating Effective Hypertext Links

To make it easier for users to navigate your Web site, the text of your hypertext links should tell readers exactly what type of document the link points to. For example, the link text

Click here for more information.

doesn't tell the user what type of document will appear when *here* is clicked. In place of phrases like *click here*, use descriptive link text such as

For more information, view our list of frequently asked questions.

If the link points to a non-HTML file, such as a PDF document, include that information in the link text. If the linked document is extremely large and will take a while to download to the user's computer, include that information in your link text so that users can decide whether or not to initiate the transfer. For example, the following link text informs users of both the type of document and its size before they initiate the link:

Download our complete manual (PDF 2 MB).

Finally, when designing the style of your Web site, make your links easy to recognize. Because most browsers underline hypertext links, don't use underlining for other text elements; use italic or boldface fonts instead. Users should never be confused about what is a link and what is not. Also, if you apply a color to your text, do not choose colors that make your hyperlinks harder to pick out against the Web page background.

You've completed your initial work linking the three files in Gerry's Web site. In the next session, you'll learn how to work with linked images and how to create links to external Web sites and Internet resources. If you want to take a break before starting the next session, you can close your files and your Web browser now.

Session 2.1 Quick Check

REVIEW

1. What is a navigation list? How would you mark up a navigation list in HTML5? How would you mark up a navigation list prior to HTML5?
2. What is a linear structure? What is a hierarchical structure?
3. What code would you enter to link the text *Sports Info* to the sports.htm file? Assume that the current document and sports.htm are in the same folder.
4. What's the difference between an absolute path and a relative path?
5. What is the purpose of the `base` element?
6. Specify the code for marking the text *CAMshots FAQ* as an `h2` heading with the id *faq*.
7. Specify the code for marking the text *Read our FAQ* as a hypertext link to an element in the current document with the id *faq*.
8. Specify the code for marking the text *Read our FAQ* as a hypertext link pointing to an element with the id *faq* in the help.htm file. Assume that help.htm lies in the same folder as the current document.

SESSION 2.2 VISUAL OVERVIEW

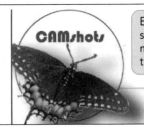

E-mail links are created by setting the href attribute to mailto:*email*, where *email* is the recipient's *e-mail* address.

To include a blank space in a link, use the %20 character entity.

Advice and News from the World of Digital Photography

Tips   Photo Glossary

```
<a href="mailto:ghayward@camshots.com?subject=CAMshots%20Message">
   contact me
</a>
```

...oto of the Month

decades o... ...tographic experience. I offer advice for both beg... ...rs and advanced users. I hope you enjoy what yo... ...d, but please be considerate of the work it took to d... ...this. The entire site contents including all image... ...d articles are copyrighted. Please honor my wo... ...d do not copy anything without permission. If... ...re interested in publishing any of my i... ...s or articles or using them in other ways, please contact me and we can discuss your needs. Happy Shoc... ...!

— Gerry

Clicking opens the link in an e-mail program, if one is available.

Colorado Double Rainbow by Watts213

- Camera: Nikon D50
- F-stop: f/7.1
- Exposure: 1/200 sec.
- Focal Length: 18mm
- Aperture: 3.6
- Flash Mode: No flash

CAM... ...s >>> ADVICE AND NEWS FROM THE WORLD OF DIGITAL PHOTOGRAPHY

```
<a href="glossary.htm#flash_mode"
   title="View Definition">
   Flash Mode
</a>:
```

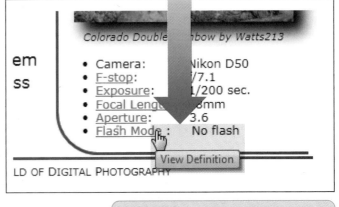

CAMshots Message - Message (HTML)

File   Message   Insert   Options   Format Text   Review

To...   ghayward@camshots.com
Cc...
Subject: CAMshots Message

A subject line can be added by appending the text string ?subject=*text* to the link, where *text* is the text of the subject line.

ghayward@camshots.com

em

ss

Colorado Double... ...bow by Watts213

- Camera: Nikon D50
- F-stop: ...f/7.1
- Exposure: 1/200 sec.
- Focal Leng... ...mm
- Aperture: ...3.6
- Flash Mod... :   No flash

View Definition

LD OF DIGITAL PHOTOGRAPHY

Use the **title** attribute to add descriptive **tooltips** to hypertext links.

IMAGE MAPS AND EXTERNAL LINKS

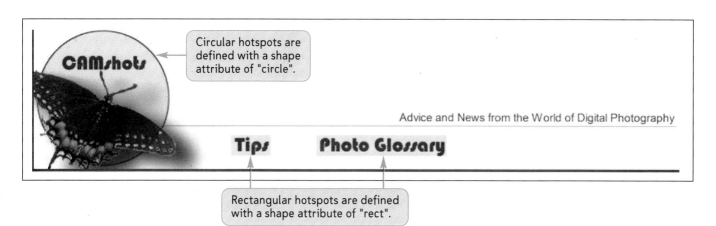

```
<img src="camshots.jpg" alt="CAMshots" usemap="#logomap" />

<map name="logomap">
    <area shape="circle" coords="82, 78,80"
     href="home.htm" alt="Home Page" />
    <area shape="rect" coords="235, 120, 310, 150"
     href="tips.htm" alt="Tips" />
    <area shape="rect" coords="340, 120, 510, 150"
     href="glossary.htm" alt="Glossary" />
</map>
```

An inline image is attached to an image map with the usemap attribute.

An **image map** maps areas called **hotspots** within an image to different linked documents.

Circular hotspots are defined with a shape attribute of "circle".

Advice and News from the World of Digital Photography

Rectangular hotspots are defined with a shape attribute of "rect".

Sample URLs to link to Internet resources

URL	Description
file:///C\server\camshots.htm	Links to the camshots.htm file in the server folder on the C drive
ftp://ftp.microsoft.com	Links to the FTP server at ftp.microsoft.com
http://www.camshots.com	Links to the Web site www.camshots.com
https://www.camshots.com	Links to the Web site www.camshots.com over a secure connection

Working with Linked Images and Image Maps

Inline images can be marked as hyperlinks using the same techniques you employed in the last session. For example, a standard practice on the Web is to turn a Web site's logo into a hyperlink pointing to the home page. This gives users quick access to the home page rather than spending time searching for a link. To mark an inline image as a hyperlink, you enclose the `<img>` tag within a set of `<a>` tags as follows:

```
<a href="reference"><img src="file" alt="text" /></a>
```

Once the image has been marked as hypertext, clicking anywhere within the image jumps the user to the linked file.

The target of the link need not be a Web page; it can also be another image file. This is commonly done for **thumbnail images** that are small representations of larger image files. Gerry has done this for his image of the photo of the month. The image on the site's home page is a thumbnail of the larger photo. Gerry wants users to be able to view the larger image file by clicking the thumbnail.

You'll turn the Photo of the Month image into a hyperlink pointing to the larger image file.

TIP

Always include alternate text for your linked images to allow non-graphical browsers to display a text link in place of the linked image.

To link the Photo of the Month image:

1. Return to the **home.htm** file in your text editor.

2. Scroll down to the `img` element for the Photo of the Month and then enclose the inline image within a set of `<a>` tags as follows (see Figure 2-29):

```
<a href="rainbow_lg.png">
   <img src="rainbow.png" alt="Photo" />
</a>
```

Figure 2-29   Linking an inline image

```
<aside>
   <h1>Photo of the Month</h1>

   <figure>
      <a href="rainbow_lg.png">
         <img src="rainbow.png" alt="Photo" />
      </a>
      <figcaption>Colorado Double Rainbow by Watts213</i></figcaption>
   </figure>
```

link to a large image of the photo

3. Save your changes to the file.

4. Reload the **home.htm** file in your Web browser. Click the Photo of the Month image and verify that the browser displays a larger, more detailed version of the image.

INSIGHT

Removing Image Borders

By default, Web browsers underline hypertext links. If an image is linked, browsers usually display the image with a colored border. To remove the border, you can add the following `style` attribute to the `img` element:

```
<img src="file" alt="text" style="border-width: 0px" />
```

This attribute sets the width of the border to 0 pixels, effectively removing it from the rendered Web page. You can also set the border width to 0 by using the following `border` attribute:

```
<img src="file" alt="text" border="0" />
```

Note that the `border` attribute is not supported in HTML5 but you will still see it used in many Web sites. Despite the fact that many browsers still support the use of the `border` attribute, you should not use it, relying instead on either the style attribute or styles set within an external style sheet.

Introducing Image Maps

When you mark an inline image as a hyperlink, the entire image is linked to the same destination file. However, HTML also allows you to divide an image into different zones, or **hotspots,** each linked to a different destination. Gerry is interested in doing this with the current image in the CAMshots header. He would like you to create hotspots for the logo so that if a user clicks anywhere within the CAMshots circle on the left side of the logo, the user jumps to the Home page; and if the user clicks either Tips or Photo Glossary in the logo, the user jumps to the Tips page or to the Glossary page, respectively. See Figure 2-30.

Figure 2-30   **Hotspots within the CAMshots header image**

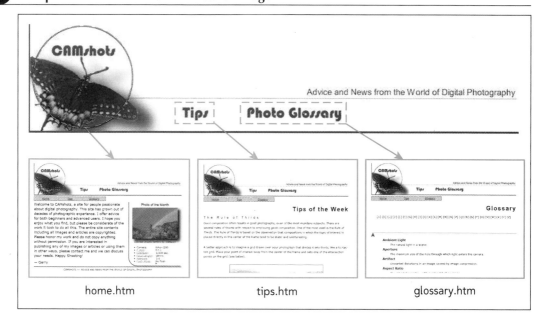

home.htm   tips.htm   glossary.htm

To define these hotspots, you create an **image map** that links a specified region of the inline image to a specific document. HTML supports two kinds of image maps: client-side image maps and server-side image maps. A **client-side image map** is an image map that is defined within the Web page and handled entirely by the Web browser running on a user's computer, while a **server-side image map** relies on a program running on the Web server to create and administer the map. For the CAMshots Web site, you'll create a client-side image map.

Client-Side Image Maps

Client-side image maps are defined with the map element

```
<map name="text">
   hotspots
</map>
```

where *text* is the name of the image map and *hotspots* are the locations of the hotspots within the image. For example, the following map element creates a client-side image map named *logomap*:

```
<map name="logomap">
   ...
</map>
```

TIP

For XHTML documents, use the id attribute in place of the name attribute to identify an image map.

Client-side image maps can be placed anywhere within the body of a Web page because they are not actually displayed by browsers, but simply used as references for mapping hotspots to inline images. The most common practice is to place a map element below the corresponding inline image.

Defining Hotspots

An individual hotspot is defined using the area element

```
<area shape="shape" coords="coordinates" href="reference"
 alt="text" />
```

where *shape* is the shape of the hotspot region, *coordinates* are the list of points that define the boundaries of the region, *reference* is the file or location that the hotspot is linked to, and *text* is alternate text displayed for non-graphical browsers. Hotspots can be created in the shapes of rectangles, circles, or polygons (multisided figures). You use a shape value of rect for rectangular hotspots, circle for circular hotspots, and poly for polygonal or multisided hotspots. A fourth possible value for the shape attribute, default, represents the remaining area of the inline image not covered by any hotspots. There is no limit to the number of hotspots you can add to an image map. Hotspots can also overlap. If they do and the user clicks an overlapping area, the browser opens the link of the first hotspot listed in the map.

Hotspot coordinates are measured in **pixels**, which are the smallest unit or dot in a digital image or display. Your computer monitor might have a size of 1024 x 768 pixels, which means that the display is 1024 dots wide by 768 dots tall. For example, the header image that Gerry uses in his Web site has dimensions of 780 pixels wide by 167 pixels tall. When used with the coords attribute of the area element, pixel values exactly define the location and size of a hotspot region.

Each hotspot shape has a different set of coordinates that define it. To define a rectangular hotspot, apply the area element

```
<area shape="rect" coords="x1, y1, x2, y2" ... />
```

where *x1, y1* are the coordinates of the upper-left corner of the rectangle and *x2, y2* are the coordinates of the rectangle's lower-right corner. Figure 2-31 shows the coordinates of the rectangular region surrounding the Photo Glossary hotspot.

| Figure 2-31 | Defining a rectangular hotspot |

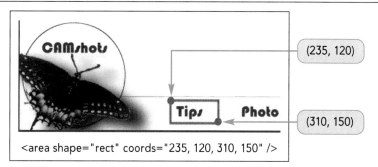

```
<area shape="rect" coords="235, 120, 310, 150" />
```

The upper-left corner of the rectangle has the image coordinates (235, 120), indicating that it is 235 pixels to the right and 120 pixels down from the upper-left corner of the image. The lower-right corner is found at the image coordinates (310, 150), placing it 310 pixels to the right and 150 pixels down from the upper-left corner of the image. Note that coordinates are always expressed relative to the upper-left corner of the image, regardless of the position of the image on the page.

Circular hotspots are defined using the coordinates

```
<area shape="circle" coords="x, y, r" ... />
```

where x and y are the coordinates of the center of the circle and r is the circle's radius. Figure 2-32 shows the coordinates for a circular hotspot around the CAMshots image from the Web site logo. The center of the circle is located at the coordinates (92, 82) and the circle has a radius of 80 pixels.

| Figure 2-32 | Defining a circular hotspot |

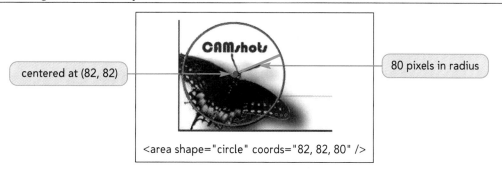

```
<area shape="circle" coords="82, 82, 80" />
```

Polygonal hotspots are defined with

```
<area shape="poly" coords="x1, y1, x2, y2, x3, y3, ..." ... />
```

where $(x1, y1)$, $(x2, y2)$, $(x3, y3)$ and so forth define the coordinates of each corner in the multisided shape. Figure 2-33 shows the coordinates for a polygonal region that covers the CAMshots logo, including the butterfly wings.

| Figure 2-33 | Defining a polygonal hotspot |

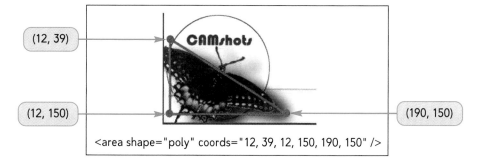

```
<area shape="poly" coords="12, 39, 12, 150, 190, 150" />
```

Finally, to define the default hotspot for an image, use

```
<area shape="default" coords="0, 0, x, y" ... />
```

where *x* is the width of the inline image in pixels and *y* is the height of the image. Any spot in an inline image that is not covered by another hotspot activates the default hotspot link.

Creating a Client-Side Image Map

- To create a client-side image map, insert the map element

```
<map name="text">
   hotspots
</map>
```

  anywhere within the Web page body, where *text* is the name of the image map and *hotspots* is a list of hotspot areas defined within the image map. (Note: For XHTML, use the id attribute in place of the name attribute.)
- To add a hotspot to the image map, place the area element

```
<area shape="shape" coords="coordinates" href="reference"
 alt="text" />
```

  within the map element, where *shape* is the shape of the hotspot region, *coordinates* is the list of points that defines the boundaries of the region, *reference* is the file or location that the hotspot is linked to, and *text* is alternate text displayed for non-graphical browsers.
- To define a rectangular-shaped hotspot, use

```
<area shape="rect" coords="x1, y1, x2, y2" ... />
```

  where *x1, y1* are the coordinates of the upper-left corner of the rectangle and *x2, y2* are the coordinates of the lower-right corner of the rectangle.
- To define a circular hotspot, use

```
<area shape="circle" coords="x, y, r" ... />
```

  where *x* and *y* are the coordinates of the center of the circle and *r* is the radius of the circle.
- To define a polygonal hotspot, use

```
<area shape="poly" coords="x1, y1, x2, y2, x3, y3, ..." ... />
```

  where (*x1, y1*), (*x2, y2*), (*x3, y3*), and so forth define the coordinates of each corner in the multisided shape.
- To define the default hotspot, use

```
<area shape="default" coords="0, 0, x, y" ... />
```

  where *x* is the width of the inline image in pixels and *y* is the height in pixels.
- To apply an image map to an inline image, add the usemap attribute

```
<img src="file" alt="text" usemap="#map" />
```

  to the inline image, where *map* is the name assigned to the image map.

To determine the coordinates of a hotspot, you can use either a graphics program such as Adobe Photoshop or image map software that automatically generates the HTML code for the hotspots you define.

In this case, assume that Gerry has already determined the coordinates for the hotspots in his image map and provided them for you. He wants you to create three hotspots, which are shown earlier in Figure 2-30. The first is a circular hotspot linked to the home.htm file, centered at the point (92, 82) and with a radius of 80 pixels. The second is a rectangular hotspot linked to the tips.htm file, with corners at (235, 120) and (310, 150). The third is also rectangular, linked to the glossary.htm file, with corners at (340, 120) and (510, 150). You do not have to create a polygonal hotspot.

You'll name the image map containing these hotspots *logomap*.

To create an image map:

1. Return to the **home.htm** file in your text editor.

2. Directly below the `<img>` tag for the CAMshots header image, insert the following map element:

```
<map name="logomap">
</map>
```

3. Within the map element, insert a circular hotspot that points to the home.htm file using the following area element:

```
<area shape="circle" coords="82, 82, 80"
 href="home.htm" alt="Home Page" />
```

4. Directly below the `<area>` tag for the circular hotspot, insert the following two rectangular hotspots pointing to the tips.htm and glossary.htm files:

```
<area shape="rect" coords="235, 120, 310, 150"
 href="tips.htm" alt="Tips" />
```

```
<area shape="rect" coords="340, 120, 510, 150"
 href="glossary.htm" alt="Glossary" />
```

Figure 2-34 highlights the new code in the file.

Figure 2-34   Creating the logomap image map

circular and rectangular hotspots →

```
<header>
    <img src="camshots.jpg" alt="CAMshots" />

    <map name="logomap">
        <area shape="circle" coords="82, 78,80"
         href="home.htm" alt="Home Page" />
        <area shape="rect" coords="235, 120, 310, 150"
         href="tips.htm" alt="Tips" />
        <area shape="rect" coords="340, 120, 510, 150"
         href="glossary.htm" alt="Glossary" />
    </map>

</header>
```

5. Save your changes to the file.

With the image map defined, your next task is to apply that map to the CAMshots header.

Applying an Image Map

To apply an image map to an image, you add the `usemap` attribute

```
<img src="file" alt="text" usemap="#map" />
```

to the inline image, where *map* is the name assigned to the image map.

Apply the *logomap* image map to the CAMshots logo and then test it in your Web browser.

To apply the *logomap* image map:

▸ **1.** Add the following attribute to the `<img>` tag for the CAMshots logo, as shown in Figure 2-35:

```
usemap="#logomap"
```

Figure 2-35 **Applying the logomap image map**

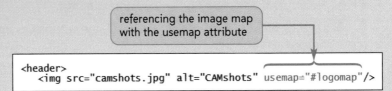

▸ **2.** Save your changes to the file and then reload or refresh the **home.htm** file in your Web browser.

▸ **3.** Click anywhere within the word **Tips** in the header image and verify that the browser opens the Tips page.

▸ **4.** Return to the home page and click anywhere within the words **Photo Glossary** in the header image to verify that the browser opens the Glossary page.

Now that you've created an image map for the logo on the home page, you can create similar image maps for the logos on the Tips and Glossary pages.

To add image maps to the other Web pages:

▸ **1.** Return to the **tips.htm** file in your text editor.

▸ **2.** Replace the code within the header element with the code shown earlier in Figure 2-34. (Hint: You can use the copy and paste feature of your text editor to copy the code from the home.htm file into the tips.htm file.)

▸ **3.** Save your changes to the file.

▸ **4.** Go to the **glossary.htm** file in your text editor.

▸ **5.** As you did for the tips.htm file, replace the code within the header element for the inline image with the code from the home.htm file. Save your changes to the file.

▸ **6.** Reload the **home.htm** file in your Web browser and verify that you can switch among the three Web pages by clicking the hotspots in the CAMshots header image.

INSIGHT

Server-Side Image Maps

The other type of image map you might encounter on the Web is a server-side image map, in which information about the hotspots is stored on the Web server rather than entered into the HTML code of a Web page. When you click a hotspot on a server-side image map, the coordinates of the mouse click are sent to the server, which activates the corresponding link, sending the linked page to your Web browser.

The server-side image map was the original HTML standard and is still supported on the Web. However, server-side maps have some limitations compared to client-side image maps. Because the map is located on the server, you need server access to test your image map code. Also, server-side image maps might be slower because information must be sent to the server with each mouse click. Finally, unlike client-side image maps, server-side image maps require the use of a mouse to send the information to the server. This makes them unsuitable for users with disabilities or users running non-graphical browsers.

To create a server-side image map, you enclose an inline image within a hypertext link such as

```
<a href="map">
    <img src="file" alt="text" ismap="ismap" />
</a>
```

where *map* is the name of a program or file running on the Web server that handles the image map. The `ismap` attribute tells the Web browser to treat the inline image as an image map.

Linking to Resources on the Internet

In the tips.htm file, Gerry has listed some of the Web sites he finds useful in his study of photography. He would like to change the entries in this list to hypertext links that his readers can click to quickly access the sites.

Introducing URLs

To create a link to a resource on the Internet, you need to know its URL. A **Uniform Resource Locator** (**URL**) specifies the location and type of a resource on the Internet. Examples of URLs include *www.whitehouse.gov*, the home page of the President of the United States, and *www.w3.org*, the home page of the World Wide Web consortium. All URLs share the general structure

```
scheme:location
```

where *scheme* indicates the type of resource referenced by the URL and *location* is the location of that resource. For Web pages, the location refers to the location of the HTML file; but for other resources, the location might simply be the name of the resource. For example, a link to an e-mail account has the recipient's e-mail address as the location.

The name of the scheme is taken from the network protocol used to access the resource. A **protocol** is a set of rules defining how information is passed between two devices. Your Web browser communicates with Web servers using the **Hypertext Transfer Protocol** (**HTTP**). Therefore, the URLs for all Web pages must start with the http scheme. Other Internet resources, described in Figure 2-36, use different communication protocols and thus have different scheme names.

Figure 2-36	Internet protocols

Protocol	Used To
file	Access documents stored locally on a user's computer
ftp	Access documents stored on an FTP server
http	Access Web pages
https	Access Web pages over a secure encrypted connection
mailto	Open a user's e-mail client and address a new message

Linking to a Web Site

The URL for a Web page has the general form

```
http://server/path/filename#id
```

where $server$ is the name of the Web server, $path$ is the path to the file on that server, $filename$ is the name of the file, and if necessary, id is the name of an id or anchor within the file. A Web page URL can also contain specific programming instructions for a browser to send to the Web server (a topic beyond the scope of this tutorial). Figure 2-37 identifies the different parts of a sample URL for a sample Web page.

Figure 2-37	Parts of a URL

You might have noticed that a URL like *http://www.camshots.com* doesn't include any pathname or filename. If a URL doesn't specify a path, then it indicates the top folder in the server's directory tree. If a URL doesn't specify a filename, the server returns the default home page. Many servers use index.html as the filename for the default home page, so the URL *http://www.camshots.com/index.html* would be equivalent to *http://www.camshots.com*.

Understanding Domain Names

The server name portion of a URL is also called the **domain name**. By studying a domain name, you learn about the server hosting the Web site. Each domain name contains a hierarchy of names separated by periods (.), with the top level appearing at the end. The top level, called an **extension**, indicates the general audience supported by the Web server. For example, *.edu* is the extension reserved for educational institutions, *.gov* is used for agencies of the United States government, and *.com* is used for commercial sites or general-use sites.

The next lower level appearing before the extension displays the name of the individual or organization hosting the site. The domain name *camshots.com* indicates a commercial or general-use site owned by CAMshots. To avoid duplicating domain names, the top two levels of the domain must be registered with the IANA (Internet Assigned Numbers Authority) before they can be used. You can usually register your domain name through your Web host. Be aware that you must pay an annual fee to keep a domain name.

The lowest levels of the domain, which appear farthest to the left in the domain name, are assigned by the individual or company hosting the site. Large Web sites involving hundreds of pages typically divide their domain names into several levels. For example, a large company like Microsoft might have one domain name for file downloads—*downloads.microsoft.com*—and another for customer service—*service.microsoft.com*. Finally, the first part of the domain name displays the name of the hard drive or resource storing the Web site files. Many companies have standardized on *www* as the initial part of their domain names.

Gerry has listed four Web pages that he wants his readers to be able to access. He's also provided you with the URLs for these pages, which are shown in Figure 2-38.

Figure 2-38 **Photography URLs**

Web Site	URL
Apogee Photo	http://www.apogeephoto.com
Outdoor Photographer	http://www.outdoorphotographer.com
Digital Photo	http://www.dpmag.com
Popular Photography and Imaging	http://www.popphoto.com

You'll link the names of the Web sites that Gerry has listed in the Tips page to the URLs listed in Figure 2-38. For example, to link the text *Apogee Photo* to the Apogee Photo Web site, you would use the following <a> tag:

```
<a href="http://www.apogeephoto.com">Apogee Photo</a>
```

Linking to Internet Resources

- The URL for a Web page is

  `http://server/path/filename#id`

  where *server* is the name of the Web server, *path* is the path to a file on that server, *filename* is the name of the file, and if necessary, *id* is the name of an id or anchor within the file.
- The URL for an FTP site is

  `ftp://server/path/filename`

  where *server* is the name of the FTP server, *path* is the folder path, and *filename* is the name of the file.
- The URL for an e-mail address is

  `mailto:address?header1=value1&header2=value2&...`

  where *address* is the e-mail address; *header1*, *header2*, etc. are different e-mail headers; and *value1*, *value2*, and so on are the values of the headers.
- The URL to reference a local file is

  `file://server/path/filename`

  where *server* is the name of the local server or computer, *path* is the path to the file on that server, and *filename* is the name of the file. If you are accessing a file on your own computer, the server name is replaced by a third slash (/).

You'll use the information that Gerry has given you to create links to all four of the Web sites listed on his Tips page.

To create links to sites on the Web:

1. Return to the **tips.htm** file in your text editor.
2. Scroll to the bottom of the file and locate the definition list containing the list of Web sites.
3. Mark the entry for Apogee Photo as a hypertext link using the following code:

   `<a href="http://www.apogeephoto.com">Apogee Photo</a>`

4. Mark the remaining three entries in the list as hypertext links pointing to each company's Web site. Figure 2-39 highlights the revised code in the file.

Figure 2-39 | **Linking to sites on the Web**

```
<article>
    <h1>Photography Sites on the Web</h1>
    <p>The Web is an excellent resource for articles on photography and
        digital cameras. Here are a few of my favorites.
    </p>

    <dl>
        <dt>&#9758;  <a href="http://www.apogeephoto.com">Apogee Photo</a></dt>
        <dd>An established online photography magazine with articles by
            top pros, discussion forums, workshops, and more.
        </dd>
        <dt>&#9758;  <a href="http://www.outdoorphotographer.com">Outdoor Photographer</a></dt>
        <dd>The premier magazine for outdoor photography. The site
            includes extensive tips on photographing wildlife, action
            sports, scenic vistas, and travel sites.
        </dd>
        <dt>&#9758;  <a href="http://www.dpmag.com">Digital Photo</a></dt>
        <dd>An excellent site for novices and professionals with
            informative reviews and buying guides for the latest equipment
            and software.
        </dd>
        <dt>&#9758;  <a href="http://www.popphoto.com">Popular Photography and Imaging</a></dt>
        <dd>A useful and informative site with articles from the
            long-established magazine of professional and amateur
            photographers.
        </dd>
    </dl>
</article>
```

▶ **5.** Save your changes to the file.

▶ **6.** Reload or refresh the **tips.htm** file in your Web browser. Figure 2-40 shows the revised list with each entry appearing as a hypertext link.

Figure 2-40 | **Links on the Tips page**

Photography   Sites   on   the   Web

The Web is an excellent resource for articles on photography and digital cameras. Here are a few of my favorites.

☞ <u>Apogee Photo</u>
An established online photography magazine with articles by top pros, discussion forums, workshops, and more.
☞ <u>Outdoor Photographer</u>
The premier magazine for outdoor photography. The site includes extensive tips on photographing wildlife, action sports, scenic vistas, and travel sites.
☞ <u>Digital Photo</u>
An excellent site for novices and professionals with informative reviews and buying guides for the latest equipment and software.
☞ <u>Popular Photography and Imaging</u>
A useful and informative site with articles from the long-established magazine of professional and amateur photographers.

▶ **7.** Click each link on the page and verify that the appropriate Web site opens.

Trouble? To open these sites, you must be connected to the Internet. If you are still having problems after connecting to the Internet, compare your code to the URLs listed in Figure 2-38 to confirm that you have not made a typing error. Also keep in mind that because the Web is constantly changing, the Web sites for some of these links might have changed, or a site might have been removed since this book was published.

Web pages are only one type of resource that you can link to. Before continuing work on the CAMshots Web site, you'll explore how to access some of these other resources.

Linking to FTP Servers

Another method of storing and sharing files on the Internet is through FTP servers. **FTP servers** are file servers that act like virtual file cabinets in which users can store and retrieve data files, much as they store files on and retrieve files from their own computers. FTP servers transfer information using a communication protocol called **File Transfer Protocol** (**FTP**). The URL to access an FTP server follows the general format

```
ftp://server/path/
```

where *server* is the name of the FTP server and *path* is the folder path on the server that contains the files you want to access. When you access an FTP site, you can navigate through its folder tree as you would navigate the folders on your own hard disk. Figure 2-41 shows an example of an FTP site viewed as a directory listing within the Internet Explorer browser, and viewed as a collection of folders that can be navigated as if they were on the user's local machine.

Figure 2-41	Accessing an FTP site over the Web

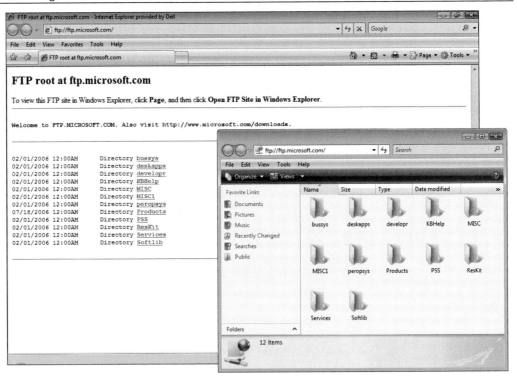

FTP servers require each user to enter a password and a username to gain access to the server's files. The standard username is *anonymous* and requires no password. Your browser supplies this information automatically, so in most situations you don't have to worry about passwords and usernames. However, some FTP servers do not allow anonymous access. In these cases, either your browser prompts you for the username and password, or you can supply a username and password within the URL using the format

```
ftp://username:password@server/path
```

where *username* and *password* are a username and password that the FTP server recognizes. It is generally *not* a good idea, however, to include usernames and passwords in URLs, as it can allow others to view your sensitive login information. It's better to let the browser send this information or to use a special program called an **FTP client**, which can encrypt or hide this information during transmission.

Linking to a Local File

HTML is a very useful language for creating collections of linked documents. Many software developers have chosen to distribute their online help in the form of HTML files. The Web sites for these help files then exist locally on a user's computer or network. If a Web site needs to reference local files (as opposed to files on the Internet or another wide area network), the URLs need to reflect this fact. The URL for a local file has the general form

```
file://server/path/filename
```

where *server* is the name of the local network server, *path* is the path on that server to the file, and *filename* is the name of the file. If you're accessing a file from your own computer, the server name can be omitted and replaced by an extra slash (/). Thus, a file from the *documents/articles* folder might have the following URL:

```
file:///documents/articles/tips.htm
```

If the file is on a different disk within your computer, the hard drive letter would be included in the URL as follows:

```
file://D:/documents/articles/tips.htm
```

Unlike the other URLs you've examined, the `file` scheme in this URL does not imply any particular communication protocol; instead, browsers retrieve the document using whatever method is the local standard for the type of file specified in the URL.

Linking to an E-Mail Address

Many Web sites use e-mail to allow users to communicate with a site's owner, sales representative, or technical support staff. You can turn an e-mail address into a hypertext link; when a user clicks the link, the user's e-mail program opens and automatically inserts the e-mail address into the *To* field of a new outgoing message. The URL for an e-mail address follows the form

```
mailto:address
```

where *address* is the e-mail address. To create a hypertext link to the e-mail address *ghayward@camshots.com*, you could use the following URL:

```
mailto:ghayward@camshots.com
```

The mailto protocol also allows you to add information to the e-mail, including the subject line and the text of the message body. To add this information to the link, you use the form

```
mailto:address?header1=value1&header2=value2&...
```

where *header1*, *header2*, etc. are different e-mail headers and *value1*, *value2*, and so on are the values of the headers. Thus, to create a link containing the e-mail message

```
TO: ghayward@camshots.com
SUBJECT: Test
BODY: This is a test message
```

you would use the following URL:

```
mailto:ghayward@camshots.com?subject=Test&Body=This%20is%20a%
20test%20message
```

Notice that the spaces in the message body *This is a test message* have been replaced with the %20 character code. This is necessary because URLs cannot contain blank spaces.

Although the mailto protocol is not technically an approved communication protocol, it is supported by almost every Web browser. However, note that a user's browser may not automatically access Web-based mail clients, such as Hotmail or Gmail, when the user clicks an e-mail link. End users accessing their mail from a Web-based mail client must configure their browsers to automatically open those Web sites in response to a mailto link.

Gerry wants you to add a link to his e-mail address on the CAMshots home page. This will give people who view his site the ability to contact him with additional questions or ideas.

To link to an e-mail address on Gerry's home page:

1. Return to the **home.htm** file in your text editor.

2. Go to the first paragraph and locate the text *contact me*.

3. Mark *contact me* as a hypertext link using the following code, as shown in Figure 2-42:

```
<a href="mailto:ghayward@camshots.com?subject=CAMshots%20Message">
   contact me
</a>
```

Figure 2-42 Linking to an e-mail address

```
<p>Welcome to CAMshots, a site for people passionate about
   digital photography. This site has grown out of decades
   of photographic experience. I offer advice for both
   beginners and advanced users. I hope you enjoy what you find,
   but please be considerate of the work it took to do all this.
   The entire site contents including all images and articles
   are copyrighted. Please honor my work and do not copy anything
   without permission. If you are interested in publishing any
   of my images or articles or using them in other ways,
   please <a href="mailto:ghayward@camshots.com?subject=CAMshots%20Message">contact me</a>
   and we can discuss your needs. Happy Shooting!</p>
<p>&mdash; Gerry</p>
```

e-mail address   e-mail subject heading

4. Save your changes to the file.

5. Refresh the **home.htm** file in your browser. Verify that the text *contact me* in the opening paragraph now appears as a hypertext link.

6. Click **contact me** and verify that your e-mail program displays a message with *ghayward@camshots.com* as the recipient and *CAMshots Message* as the subject.

    Trouble? If you are using a Web-based e-mail client such as Gmail or Hotmail, the browser will not open your e-mail client. You can view online documentation for your browser to determine whether it supports linking to Web-based e-mail clients.

7. Close your message window without saving the message.

Problem Solving: E-Mail Links and Spam

Use caution when adding e-mail links to your Web site. While it may make it more convenient for users to contact you, it also might make you more vulnerable to spam. **Spam** is unsolicited e-mail sent to large numbers of people, promoting products, services, and in some cases inappropriate Web sites. Spammers create their e-mail lists by scanning discussion groups, stealing Internet mailing lists, and using programs called **e-mail harvesters** to scan HTML code for the e-mail addresses contained in mailto URLs. Many Web developers have removed e-mail links from their Web sites in order to foil these harvesters, replacing the links with Web forms that submit e-mail requests to a secure server. If you need to include an e-mail address as a link on your Web page, you can take a few steps to reduce your exposure to spammers:

- Replace the text of the e-mail addresses with inline images that are more difficult for e-mail harvesters to read.
- Write a program to scramble any e-mail addresses in the HTML code, unscrambling the e-mail address only when a user clicks it.
- Replace the characters of the e-mail address with escape characters. For example, you can replace the @ symbol with the escape sequence %40.

There is no quick and easy solution to this problem. Fighting spammers is an ongoing battle, and they have proved very resourceful in overcoming some of the defenses people have created. As you develop your Web site, you should carefully consider how to handle e-mail addresses and review the most current methods for safeguarding that information.

Working with Hypertext Attributes

HTML provides several attributes to control the behavior and appearance of your links. Gerry suggests that you study a few of these to see whether they would be effective in his Web site.

Opening a Secondary Window or Tab

By default, each page you open replaces the contents of the current page in the browser window. This means that when Gerry's readers click on one of the four external links listed on the Tips page, they leave the CAMshots Web site. To return to the Web site, a user would have to click the browser's Back button.

Gerry wants his Web site to stay open when a user clicks one of the links to the external Web sites. Most browsers allow users to open multiple browser windows or multiple tabs within the same browser window. Gerry suggests that links to external sites be opened in a second browser window or tab. This arrangement allows continual access to his Web site, even as users are browsing other sites.

To force a document to appear in a new window or tab, you add the `target` attribute to the <a> tag. The general syntax is

```
<a href="url" target="window">content</a>
```

where `window` is a name assigned to the new browser window or browser tab. The value you use for the `target` attribute doesn't affect the appearance or content of the page being opened; the target simply identifies the different windows or tabs that are currently open. You can choose any name you wish for the target. If several links have the same target name, they all open in the same location, replacing the previous content in the browser window or tab. HTML also supports the special target names described in Figure 2-43.

Figure 2-43 | **Target names for browser windows and tabs**

Target Name	Description
target	Opens the link in a new window or tab named *target*
_blank	Opens the link in a new, unnamed window or tab
_self	Opens the link in the current browser window or tab

Whether the new page is opened in a tab or in a browser window is determined by the browser settings. It cannot be set by the HTML code.

REFERENCE

Opening a Link in a New Window or Tab

- To open a link in a new browser window or browser tab, add the attribute

  ```
  target="window"
  ```

  to the <a> tag, where *window* is a name assigned to the new browser window or tab. The target attribute can also be set to _blank for a new, unnamed browser window or tab, or to _self for the current browser window or tab.

Gerry suggests that all of the external links from his page be opened in a browser window or tab identified with the target name *new*.

To specify a link target:

1. Return to the **tips.htm** file in your text editor.

2. Scroll to the bottom of the file and locate the four links to the external Web sites.

3. Within each of the opening <a> tags, insert the following attribute, as shown in Figure 2-44:

   ```
   target="new"
   ```

Figure 2-44 | **Setting a target for hyperlinks**

```
<dl>
    <dt>&#9758; <a href="http://www.apogeephoto.com" target="new">Apogee Photo</a></dt>
    <dd>An established online photography magazine with articles by
        top pros, discussion forums, workshops, and more.
    </dd>
    <dt>&#9758; <a href="http://www.outdoorphotographer.com" target="new">Outdoor Photographer</a></dt>
    <dd>The premier magazine for outdoor photography. The site
        includes extensive tips on photographing wildlife, action
        sports, scenic vistas, and travel sites.
    </dd>
    <dt>&#9758; <a href="http://www.dpmag.com" target="new">Digital Photo</a></dt>
    <dd>An excellent site for novices and professionals with
        informative reviews and buying guides for the latest equipment
        and software.
    </dd>
    <dt>&#9758; <a href="http://www.popphoto.com" target="new">Popular Photography and Imaging</a></dt>
    <dd>A useful and informative site with articles from the
        long-established magazine of professional and amateur
        photographers.
    </dd>
</dl>
</article>
```

4. Save your changes to the file.

5. Refresh the **tips.htm** file in your browser. Click each of the four links to external Web sites and verify that each opens in the same new browser window or tab.

6. Close the secondary browser window or tab.

You should use the `target` attribute sparingly in your Web site. Creating secondary windows can clutter up a user's desktop. Also, because the page is placed in a new window, users cannot use the Back button to return to the previous page in that window; they must click the browser's program button or the tab for the original Web site. This confuses some users and annoys others. Many Web designers now advocate not using the target attribute at all, leaving the choice of opening a link in a new tab or window to users. Note that the target attribute is not supported in strict XHTML-compliant code.

Creating a Tooltip

If you want to provide additional information about a link on your Web page, you can add a tooltip to the link. A **tooltip** is descriptive text that appears when a user positions the mouse pointer over a link. Figure 2-45 shows an example of a tooltip applied to one of Gerry's links.

Figure 2-45 **Viewing a tooltip**

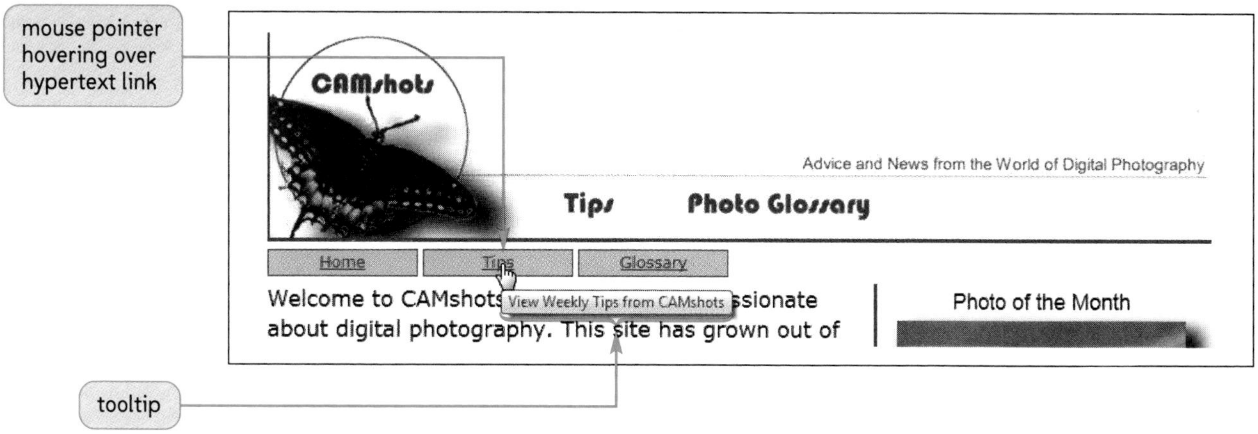

To create the tooltip, add the title attribute to the opening <a> tag in the form

```
<a href="url" title="text">content</a>
```

where *text* is the text that appears in the tooltip. To create the tooltip shown in Figure 2-45, you would enter the following HTML code:

```
<a href="tips.htm"
    title="View Weekly Tips from CAMshots">
    Tips
</a>
```

Tooltips can also be added to image map hotspots to provide more useful feedback to the user.

Creating a Semantic Link

The text of a hypertext link should always describe to users the type of document that the link opens. You can also use the `rel` attribute to indicate the type of document that a link calls. For example, in the links to the site's home page, Gerry could insert the following `rel` attribute, setting its value to *first* to indicate that the home page is the first document in the CAMshots Web site:

```
<a href="home.htm" rel="first">Home Page</a>
```

A hypertext link containing the `rel` attribute is called a **semantic link** because the tag contains information about the relationship between the link and its destination. This information is not intended for the user, but for the browser. For example, a browser could be set up to mark the first Web page in a site with a special icon or to provide scripts that allow quick access to a site's first page.

Although the `rel` attribute is not limited to a fixed set of values, the specifications for HTML and XHTML include a proposed list of special values. Figure 2-46 shows some of these proposed relationship values.

| Figure 2-46 | Proposed values for the rel attribute |

rel Attribute	Link To ...
alternate	An alternate version of the document
archives	A collection of historical documents
author	Information about the author of the document
external	An external document
first	The first document in a selection
help	A help document
index	An index for the document
last	The last document in a selection
license	Copyright information for the document
next	The next document in a selection
prev	The previous document in a selection
search	A search tool for the selection
sidebar	A document that should be shown in the browser's sidebar
stylesheet	An external style sheet

HTML 4.01 and XHTML also support the `rev` attribute to describe the reverse relationship: how a linked document views the current document. For example, if you're linking to the Glossary page from the home page, the reverse relation is *first* (because that is how the Glossary page views the home page). The HTML code would be

```
<a href="glossary.htm" rel="glossary" rev="first">Glossary</a>
```

The `rev` attribute is not supported in HTML5.

At this point, Gerry decides against using the `rel` and `rev` attributes on his Web site. However, he'll keep them in mind as an option as his Web site expands in size and complexity.

Using the `link` Element

Another way to add a hypertext link to your document is to add a `link` element to the document's head with the syntax

```
<link href="url" rel="text" rev="text" target="window" />
```

where the *href*, *rel*, *rev*, and *target* attributes serve the same purpose as in the `<a>` tag. You've already used the `link` element to link your Web pages to external style sheets, but you can use it to link to other types of documents as well. For example, to use the `link` element to create semantic links to the three pages of Gerry's Web site, you could add the following link elements to the `head` element of each document:

```
<link rel="first" href="home.htm" />
<link rel="help" href="tips.htm" />
<link rel="index" href="glossary.htm" />
```

Because they are placed within a document's head, `link` elements do not appear as part of the Web page. Instead, if a browser supports it, the links can be displayed in a browser toolbar. The advantage of the `link` element used in this way is that it places the list of links outside of the Web page, freeing up page space for other content. Also, because the links appear in a browser toolbar, they are always easily accessible to users. Currently, Opera is one of the few browsers with built-in support for the `link` element. Third-party software exists to provide this support for Internet Explorer and Firefox. Because no single list of relationship names is widely accepted, you must check with each browser's documentation to find out what relationship names it supports. Until semantic links are embraced by more browsers, you should use them only if you duplicate that information elsewhere on the page.

Working with Metadata

Gerry is happy with the work you've done on the design for his CAMshots Web site. Now he wants to start working on getting the site noticed. When someone searches for "digital photography tips" or "camera buying guide," will they find Gerry's Web site? There are thousands of photography sites on the Web. Gerry knows he needs to add a few extra touches to his home page to make it more likely that the site will be picked up by major search engines such as Yahoo! and Google.

Optimizing a Web site for search engines can be a long and involved process. For the best results, Web authors often turn to **search engine optimization** (**SEO**) tools to make their sites appear more prominently in search engines. Because CAMshots is a hobby site, Gerry does not want to invest any money in improving the site's visibility; but he would like to do a few simple things that would help.

Using the `meta` Element

To be noticed on the Web, a site needs to include information about itself for search engines to read and add to their search indices. Information about a site is called **metadata**. You can add metadata to your Web pages by adding a `meta` element to the document head. In the last tutorial, you saw how to use the `meta` element to store information about the character set used by the page; but you can also use it to store other information about the document. The syntax of the `meta` element is

```
<meta name="text" content="text" scheme="text" http-equiv="text" />
```

where the `name` attribute specifies the type of metadata, the `content` attribute stores the metadata value, the `scheme` attribute defines the metadata format, and the `http-equiv` attribute is used to attach metadata or commands to the communication stream between the Web server and the browser. Note that the `scheme` attribute is not supported under HTML5, while the `charset` attribute (not listed above) is supported only under HTML5.

There are three uses of the `meta` element:

- To store information about a document that can be read by the author, other users, and Web browsers
- To control how browsers handle a document, including forcing browsers to automatically refresh the page at timed intervals
- To assist Web search engines in adding a document to their search index

For example, the following `meta` element stores the name of the Web page's author:

```
<meta name="author" content="Gerry Hayward" />
```

For search engines, you should include metadata describing the site and the topics it covers. This is done by adding a `meta` element containing the site description and another meta element with a list of keywords. The following two elements would summarize the CAMshots Web site for search engines:

```
<meta name="description" content="CAMshots provides advice on
digital cameras and photography" />

<meta name="keywords" content="photography, cameras, digital
imaging" />
```

Figure 2-47 lists some other examples of metadata that you can use to describe your documents.

Figure 2-47   **Examples of the uses of the meta element**

Meta Name	Example	Description
author	`<meta name="author" content="Gerry Hayward" />`	Supplies the name of the document author
classification	`<meta name="classification" content="photography" />`	Classifies the document category
copyright	`<meta name="copyright" content="&copy; 2014 CAMshots" />`	Provides a copyright statement
description	`<meta name="description" content="Digital photography and advice" />`	Provides a description of the document
generator	`<meta name="generator" content="Dreamweaver" />`	Indicates the name of the program that created the HTML code for the document
keywords	`<meta name="keywords" content="photography, cameras, digital imaging" />`	Provides a list of keywords describing the document
owner	`<meta name="owner" content="CAMshots" />`	Indicates the owner of the document
rating	`<meta name="rating" content="general" />`	Provides a rating of the document in terms of its suitability for minors
reply-to	`<meta name="reply-to" content="ghayward@camshots.com (G. Hayward)" />`	Supplies a contact e-mail address and name for the document

In recent years, search engines have become more sophisticated in evaluating Web sites. In the process, the `meta` element has decreased in importance. However, it is still used by search engines when adding a site to their indices. Because adding metadata requires very little effort, you should still include `meta` elements in your Web documents.

REFERENCE

Working with Metadata

- To document the contents of a Web page, use the meta element

  ```
  <meta name="text" content="text" />
  ```

  where the `name` attribute specifies the type of metadata and the `content` attribute stores the metadata value.
- To add metadata or a command to the communication stream between the Web server and Web browsers, use

  ```
  <meta http-equiv="text" content="text" />
  ```

  where the `http-equiv` attribute specifies the type of data or command attached to the communication stream and the content attribute specifies the data value or command.

Having discussed metadata issues with you, Gerry asks that you include a few `meta` elements to describe his new site.

To add metadata to Gerry's document:

1. Return to the **home.htm** file in your text editor.

2. Directly below the `meta` element that defines the document's character set, insert the following `meta` elements, as shown in Figure 2-48:

```
<meta name="author" content="your name" />
<meta name="description" content="A site for sharing information on
digital photography and cameras" />
<meta name="keywords" content="photography, cameras, digital
imaging" />
```

Figure 2-48   Adding meta elements to the CAMshots home page

```
<meta charset="UTF-8" />
<meta name="author" content="Gerry Hayward" />
<meta name="description" content="A site for sharing information on
                digital photography and cameras" />
<meta name="keywords" content="photography, cameras, digital imaging" />

<title>CAMshots Home Page</title>
<script src="modernizr-1.5.js"></script>
<link href="camstyles.css" rel="stylesheet" type="text/css" />
</head>
```

metadata category

metadata value

3. Close the file, saving your changes.

4. Close any open files or applications.

Using the meta Element to Reload a Web Page

Describing your document is not the only use of the meta element. As you learned earlier, servers transmit Web pages using a communication protocol called HTTP. You can add information and commands to this communication stream with the http-equiv attribute of the meta element. One common use of the http-equiv attribute is to force browsers to refresh a Web page at timed intervals, which is useful for Web sites that publish scoreboards or stock tickers. For example, to automatically refresh a Web page every 60 seconds, you would apply the following meta element:

```
<meta http-equiv="refresh" content="60" />
```

Another use of the meta element is to redirect the browser from the current document to a new document. This might prove useful to Gerry someday if he changes the URL of his site's home page. As his readers get accustomed to the new Web address, he can keep the old address online, automatically redirecting readers to the new site. The meta element to perform an automatic redirect has the general form

```
<meta http-equiv="refresh" content="sec;url=url" />
```

TIP

When redirecting a Web site to a new URL, avoid confusion by always including text notifying users that the page is being redirected, and provide users several seconds to read the text.

where *sec* is the time in seconds before the browser redirects the user and *url* is the URL of the new site. To redirect users after five seconds to the Web page at *http://www. camshots.com*, you could enter the following meta element:

```
<meta http-equiv="refresh" content="5;url=http://www.camshots.com" />
```

At this point, Gerry does not need to use the meta element to send data or commands through the HTTP communication protocol. However, he will keep this option in mind if he moves the site to a new address.

Gerry is happy with the Web site you've started. He'll continue to work on the site and will come back to you for more assistance as he adds new pages and elements.

REVIEW

Session 2.2 Quick Check

1. The CAMmap image map has a circular hotspot centered at the point (50, 75) with a radius of 40 pixels pointing to the faq.htm file. Specify the code to create a map element containing this circular hotspot.

2. An inline image based on the logo.jpg file with the alternate text *CAMshots* needs to use the CAMmap image map. Specify the code to apply the image map to the image.

3. What are the five parts of a URL?

4. Specify the code to link the text *White House* to the URL *http://www. whitehouse.gov*, with the destination document displayed in a new unnamed browser window.

5. Specify the code to link the text *University of Washington* to the FTP server at *ftp.uwash.edu*.

6. Specify the code to link the text *President of the United States* to the e-mail address *president@whitehouse.gov*.

7. What attribute would you add to a hypertext link to display the tooltip *Tour the White House*?

8. Specify the code to add the description *United States Office of the President* as metadata to a document.

9. Specify the code to automatically refresh your Web document every 5 minutes.

Practice the skills you learned in the tutorial using the same case scenario.

PRACTICE

Review Assignments

Data Files needed for the Review Assignments: camhome.htm, child1.jpg–child3.jpg, childtxt.htm, conlogo.jpg, constyles.css, contest1.png–contest3.png, contesttxt.htm, flower1.jpg–flower3.jpg, flowertxt.htm, modernizr-1.5.js, photogloss.htm, scenic1.jpg–scenic3.jpg, scenictxt.htm, thirdstip.jpg, thumb1.jpg–thumb9.jpg, tipweek.htm

Gerry has been working on the CAMshots Web site for a while. During that time, the site has grown in popularity with amateur photographers. Now he wants to host a monthly photo contest to highlight the work of his colleagues. Each month Gerry will pick the three best photos from different photo categories. He's asked for your help in creating the collection of Web pages highlighting the winning entries. Gerry has already created four pages. The first page contains information about the photo contest; the remaining three pages contain the winning entries for child photos, scenic photos, and flower photos. Although Gerry has already entered much of the page content, he needs you to work on creating the links between and within each page. Figure 2-49 shows a preview of the photo contest's home page.

| Figure 2-49 | CAMshots Contest Winners page |

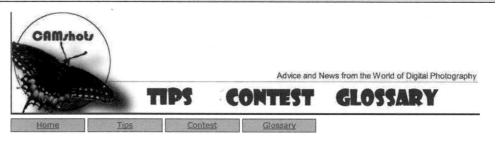

Contest Winners

Here are the results for this month's contest in the categories of *Child Photos*, *Flower Photos*, and *Scenic Photos*. I received hundreds of entries and it was difficult to narrow the entries down to three in each category. Thanks to everyone who participated this month.

Below are thumbnail images of the winning photos. You can click the photos to view larger images of each. These photos are distributed for non-commercial use. If you wish to obtain copies for commercial use, please contact the photographer.

Next Month's Contest Categories

- Animal Photos
- Nighttime Photos
- Sports Photos

Please submit your entries to Gerry Hayward. Include your name, the photo category, and the photo settings. JPEG photos only.

Attention: Our friends at BetterPhoto.com are having their annual photo contest. Please take this opportunity to submit your work to their editors.

Child Photos

Flower Photos

Scenic Photos

Complete the following:

1. Use your text editor to open the **contesttxt.htm**, **childtxt.htm**, **scenictxt.htm**, and **flowertxt.htm** files from the tutorial.02\review folder included with your Data Files. Enter *your name* and *the date* within each file, and then save them as **contest.htm**, **child.htm**, **scenic.htm**, and **flower.htm**, respectively, in the same folder.

2. Go to the **child.htm** file in your text editor. Directly below the `header` element, create a navigation list containing an unordered list with the following list items as hyperlinks:

   a. **Home** linked to the camhome.htm file

   b. **Tips** linked to the tipweek.htm file

   c. **Contest** linked to the contest.htm file

   d. **Glossary** linked to the photogloss.htm file

3. Go to the `section` element and locate the contest1.png inline image. Directly below the inline image, insert an image map with the following properties:

   a. Set the name of the image map as **contestmap**.

   b. Add a polygonal hotspot pointing to the child.htm file containing the points (427, 5), (535, 20), (530, 59), and (421, 43). Enter **Child Photos** as the alternate text for the hotspot.

   c. Add a polygonal hotspot pointing to the flower.htm file containing the points (539, 57), (641, 84), (651, 46), and (547, 26). Enter **Flower Photos** as the alternate text for the hotspot.

   d. Add a polygonal hotspot pointing to the scenic.htm file containing the points (650, 86), (753, 125), (766, 78), and (662, 49). Enter **Scenic Photos** as the alternate text for the hotspot.

4. Apply the contestmap image map to the contest1 inline image.

5. Locate the three `h2` elements naming the three child photo winners. Assign the `h2` elements the ids **photo1**, **photo2**, and **photo3**, respectively.

6. Save your changes to the file.

7. Go to the **flower.htm** file in your text editor. Repeat Steps 2 through 6, applying the image map to the contest2.png image at the top of the `section` element.

8. Go to the **scenic.htm** file in your text editor. Repeat Steps 2 through 6 applying the image map to the contest3.png image at the top of the `section` element.

9. Go to the **contest.htm** file in your text editor. Repeat Step 2 to insert a navigation list at the top of the page.

10. Scroll down to the second article. Link the text *Child Photos* to the child.htm file. Link *Flower Photos* to the flower.htm file. Link *Scenic Photos* to the scenic.htm file.

11. Scroll down to the nine thumbnail images (named *thumb1.jpg* through *thumb9.jpg*). Link each inline image to the corresponding `h2` heading in the child.htm, flower.htm, or scenic.htm file you identified in Step 5.

12. Scroll down to the aside element. Mark the text *Gerry Hayward* as a hypertext link to an e-mail address with **ghayward@camshots.com** as the e-mail address and **Photo Contest** as the subject line.

13. Mark the text *BetterPhoto.com* as a hypertext link pointing to the URL **http://www.betterphoto.com**. Set the attribute of the link so that it opens in a new browser window or tab.

14. Save your changes to the file.

15. Open **contest.htm** in your Web browser. Verify that the e-mail link opens a new mail message window with the subject line *Photo Contest*. Verify that the link to BetterPhoto.com opens that Web site in a new browser window or tab. Verify that you can navigate through the Web site using the hypertext links in the navigation list. Finally, click each of the nine thumbnail images at the bottom of the page and verify that each connects to the larger image of the photo on the appropriate photo contest page.

16. Go to the **child.htm** file in your Web browser. Verify that you can navigate forward and backward through the three photo contest pages by clicking the hotspots in the image map.

17. Submit your completed files to your instructor, in either printed or electronic form, as requested.

Apply your knowledge of hypertext links to create a directory of universities and colleges.

APPLY

Case Problem 1

Data Files needed for this Case Problem: colleges.txt, hestyles.css, highered.jpg, modernizr-1.5.js, uwlisttxt.htm

HigherEd   Adella Coronel is a guidance counselor for Eagle High School in Waunakee, Wisconsin. She wants to take her interest in helping students choose colleges to the Web by starting a Web site called HigherEd. She's come to you for help in creating the site. The first page she wants to create is a simple directory of Wisconsin colleges and universities. She's created the list of schools, but has not yet marked the entries in the list as hypertext links. The list is very long, so she has broken it down into three categories: private colleges and universities, technical colleges, and public universities. Because of the length of the page, she wants to include hypertext links that allow students to jump down to a specific college category. Figure 2-50 shows a preview of the page you'll create for Adella.

Figure 2-50   **HigherEd Web site**

Higher ◆ Ed

The Directory of Higher Education Opportunities

Wisconsin Colleges and Universities

| Private Colleges and Universities | Technical College System | University of Wisconsin System |

Private Colleges and Universities

  Alverno College
  Beloit College
  Cardinal Stritch University
  Carroll College
  Concordia University Wisconsin
  Edgewood College
  Lakeland College
  Lawrence University
  Marian University
  Medical College of Wisconsin
  Milwaukee Institute of Art and Design
  Milwaukee School of Engineering

Complete the following:

1. In your text editor, open the **uwlisttxt.htm** file from the tutorial.02\case1 folder included with your Data Files. Enter *your name* and *the date* in the file comments. Save the file as **uwlist.htm** in the same folder.

2. Directly below the h1 heading, insert a navigation list containing an unordered list with following list items: **Private Colleges and Universities**, **Technical College System**, and **University of Wisconsin System**.

3. Add the ids **private**, **technical**, and **public** to the three h2 headings that categorize the list of schools.

4. Mark each of the school entries on the page as a hypertext link. Use the URLs provided in the colleges.txt file. (Hint: Use the copy and paste feature of your text editor to efficiently copy and paste the URL text.)

⊕ EXPLORE 5. Adella wants the links to the school Web sites to appear in a new tab or window. Because there are so many links on the page, add a base element to the document head specifying that all links open by default in a new browser window or tab named **collegeWin**.

6. Link the three items in your navigation list to the corresponding h2 headings.

⊕ EXPLORE 7. For each of the hypertext links you marked in Step 6, set the link to open in the current browser window and not in a new browser window or tab.

8. Save your changes to the file.

9. Open **uwlist.htm** in your Web browser and verify that the school links all open in the same browser window or tab, and that the links within the document to the different school categories bring the user to those locations on the page but not in a new window or tab.

10. Submit your completed files to your instructor, in either printed or electronic form, as requested.

Apply your knowledge of HTML to create a slide show Web site.

APPLY

Case Problem 2

Data Files needed for this Case Problem: fiddler.jpg, fidstyles.css, first.png, home.png, hometxt.htm, last.png, modernizr-1.5.js, next.png, prev.png, slide1.jpg–slide6.jpg, slide1txt.htm–slide6txt.htm, thumb1.jpg–thumb6.jpg

Lakewood School Tasha Juroszek is a forensics teacher at Lakewood School, a small private school in Moultrie, Georgia. Tasha has just finished directing her students in *Fiddler on the Roof, Jr.* and wants to place a slide show of the performances on the Web. She has already designed the layout and content of the pages, but needs help to finish the slide show. She has asked you to add hypertext links between the slide pages and the site's home page. Figure 2-51 shows a preview of one of the slide pages on the Web site.

Figure 2-51   Fiddler on the Roof, Jr. slide page

If I Were a Rich Man sung by T. Gates

Complete the following:

1. Use your text editor to open the **hometxt.htm** file and the **slide1txt.htm** through **slide6txt.htm** files from the tutorial.02\case2 folder included with your Data Files. Enter *your name* and *the date* in the comment section of each file. Save the files as **home.htm** and **slide1.htm** through **slide6.htm**, respectively.

2. Return to the **slide1.htm** file in your text editor. At the top of the page are five buttons used to navigate through the slide show. Locate the inline image for the home button (home.png) and mark it as a hypertext link pointing to the home.htm file. Add the tooltip **Home Page** to the hyperlink.

3. There are six slides in Tasha's slide show. Mark the First Slide button as a hypertext link pointing to the slide1.htm file. Mark the Last Slide button as a link to the slide6.htm file. Link the Previous Slide button to slide1.htm, the first slide in the show. Link the Next Slide button to the slide2.htm file. Add an appropriate tooltip to each hyperlink.

4. Directly below the slide show buttons are thumbnail images of the six slides. Link each thumbnail image to its slide page.

5. Save your changes to the file.

6. Repeat Steps 2 through 5 for the five remaining slide pages. Within each page, set the navigation buttons to go back and forth through the slide show. For the slide6.htm file, the Next Slide button should point to the slide6.htm file because it is the last slide in the show.

7. Go to the **home.htm** file in your text editor. Go to the first paragraph in the article and mark the text string *slide show* as a hypertext link pointing to the slide1.htm file.

8. Go to the end of the second paragraph and mark the phrase *contact me* as a hypertext link pointing to the e-mail address **tashajur@lakewood.edu**, with the subject heading **Digital Photo**.

9. Save your changes to the file.

10. Load the **home.htm** file in your Web browser. Test the links in the Web site and verify that they allow the user to easily move back and forth through the slide show.

11. Submit your completed files to your instructor, in either printed or electronic form, as requested.

Explore how to use HTML to create an election results Web site.

CHALLENGE

Case Problem 3

Data Files needed for this Case Problem: dcoords.txt, dist1txt.htm–dist4txt.htm, ewlogo.png, ewstyles.css, kansasmap.png, kansastxt.htm, modernizr-1.5.js

ElectionWeb Allison Hawks is a political science student at the University of Kansas. As part of a project for one of her courses, she is setting up a Web site to report results from the upcoming elections. She's asked for your help in designing and writing the hypertext links and image maps to be used throughout her site. She has created a set of sample files detailing hypothetical results for the races for governor, senator, and the four Kansas congressional districts. A preview of the site's home page is shown in Figure 2-52.

Figure 2-52	Kansas results from ElectionWeb

Kansas Statewide Races

News Sources

- Yahoo! News
- FOX News
- CNN
- MSNBC
- Google News
- New York Times
- digg
- Washington Post
- LATimes
- Reuters
- ABCNews
- USA Today

The Kansas Election polls have officially been closed now for two hours and results are being constantly updated. As of 10pm with 65% of the ballots counted, leaders in the state-wide races for governor and senator are as follows:

Governor (65% reporting)

Charles Young (R) - 371,885 (47%)
Karen Drew (D) - 356,060 (45%)
Barry Davis (I) - 39,562 (5%)

U.S. Senate (65% reporting)

✔ Helen Sanchez (D) - 387,710 (49%)
Linda Epstein (R) - 348,147 (44%)
Hunter Ryan (I) - 47,474 (6%)

Get up-to-the-minute election results from the Kansas Secretary of State.

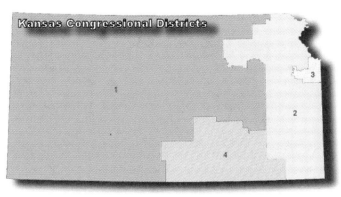

Click to view congressional district results

ElectionWeb: *Your Source for Online Election Results*

Complete the following:

1. Use your text editor to open the **kansastxt.htm** file and the **dist1txt.htm** through **dist4txt.htm** files from the tutorial.02\case3 folder included with your Data Files. Enter **your name** and **the date** in the comment section of each file. Save the files as **kansas.htm** and **district1.htm** through **district4.htm,** respectively.

⊕ EXPLORE

2. Go to the **kansas.htm** file in your text editor. Use the `meta` element to specify **your name** as the document author, and **Kansas** and **elections** as keywords for Web search engines.

⊕ EXPLORE

3. Create a semantic link in the document head linking this document to the Office of the Kansas Secretary of State at the following address:
   http://www.kssos.org/elections/elections_statistics.html
   Use a `rel` attribute value of **external** for the link.

4. Set the base target of the Web page to **new** so that links on the page open, by default, in a new browser window or tab.

5. Go to the page body, and then directly below the header element insert a navigation list with the following content:

   a. An h2 heading with the text **News Sources**

   b. An unordered list containing the following entries: **Yahoo! News**, **FOX News**, **CNN**, **MSNBC**, **Google News**, **New York Times**, **digg**, **Washington Post**, **LATimes**, **Reuters**, **ABCNews**, and **USA Today**.

   c. Look up the Web addresses of the 12 news sources and link your list entries to the appropriate Web sites. Set the rel attribute of each link to **external**.

6. Scroll down to the last paragraph before the figure box and link the text *Secretary of State* to the Office of the Kansas Secretary of State Web site.

7. Directly below the figure box, create an image map named **kansasdistricts** containing four polygonal hotspots for each of the four Kansas congressional districts. Use the coordinates found in the dcoords.txt file as the coordinates of the hotspots.

⊕ EXPLORE

8. Set the hotspots in your image map to access the district1.htm, district2.htm, district3.htm, and district4.htm files, using the target attribute value of **_self** so that those Web pages open within the current browser window or tab.

9. Apply the kansasdistricts image map to the kansasmap.png inline image.

10. Save your changes to the file.

11. Go to the **district1.htm** file in your text editor.

12. Directly below the opening `<section>` tag, insert a navigation list containing an unordered list with the items **District 1**, **District 2**, **District 3**, and **District 4**. Link each entry to its corresponding Web page in the ElectionWeb Web site.

13. Scroll down to the last paragraph before the figure box and link the text *statewide races* to the kansas.htm file.

14. Apply the same image map you created in Step 7 for the kansas.htm file to the kansasmap.png inline image.

15. Save your changes to the file.

16. Open the **district2.htm**, **district3.htm**, and **district4.htm** files in your text editor and repeat Steps 12 through 15 for each file.

17. Open the **kansas.htm** file in your Web browser and verify that you can navigate through Allison's sample pages by clicking the hypertext links within the page body and within the image maps. Verify that you can access the external Web sites listed in the news sources and the Office of the Kansas Secretary of State.

18. Submit your completed project to your instructor, in either printed or electronic form, as requested.

Test your knowledge of HTML and use your creativity to design a Web site documenting a Shakespeare play.

RESEARCH

Case Problem 4

Data Files needed for this Case Problem: characters.txt, notes.txt, tempest.jpg, tempest.txt

Mansfield Classical Theatre Steve Karls continues to work as the director of Mansfield Classical Theatre in Mansfield, Ohio. The next production he plans to direct is *The Tempest*. Steve wants to put the text of this play on the Web, but he also wants to augment the dialog of the play with notes and commentary. However, he doesn't want his commentary to get in the way of a straight-through reading of the text, so he has hit on the idea of linking his commentary to key phrases in the dialog. Steve has created text files containing an excerpt from *The Tempest* as well as his commentary and other supporting documents. He would like you to take his raw material and create a collection of linked pages.

Complete the following:

1. Create HTML files named **tempest.htm**, **commentary.htm**, and **cast.htm**, saving them in the tutorial.02\case4 folder included with your Data Files. Add comment tags to the head section of each document containing your name and the date. Add an appropriate page title to each document.

2. Using the contents of the tempest.txt, notes.txt, and characters.txt text files, create the body of the three Web pages in Steve's Web site. You can supplement the material on the page with appropriate material you find on your own.

3. Use the tempest.jpg file as a logo for the page. Create an image map from the logo pointing to the tempest.htm, commentary.htm, and cast.htm files. The three rectangular boxes on the logo have the following coordinates for their upper-left and lower-right corners:

   The Play: (228, 139) (345, 173)

   Commentary: (359, 139) (508, 173)

   The Cast: (520, 139) (638, 173)

4. Use this image map in all three of the Web pages for this Web site.

5. Create links between the dialog on the play page and the notes on the commentary page. The notes contain line numbers to aid you in linking each line of dialog to the appropriate note.

6. Create a link between the first appearance of each character's name in the tempest. htm page and the character's description on the cast.htm page.

7. Include a link to Steve Karls' e-mail address on the tempest.htm page. Steve's e-mail address is **stevekarls@mansfieldct.com**. E-mail sent to Steve's account from this Web page should have the subject line **Comments on the Tempest**.

8. Add appropriate `meta` elements to each of the three pages documenting the page's contents and purpose.

9. Search the Web for sites that would provide additional material about the play. Add links to these pages on the tempest.htm page. The links should open in a new browser window or tab.

10. Submit your completed files to your instructor, in either printed or electronic form, as requested.

ENDING DATA FILES

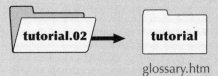

tutorial

glossary.htm
home.htm
tips.htm
+ 1 style sheet
+ 5 graphic files
modernizr-1.5.js

review

camhome.htm
child.htm
contest.htm
flower.htm
photogloss.htm
scenic.htm
tipweek.htm
+ 1 style sheet
+ 23 graphic files
modernizr-1.5.js

case1

uwlist.htm
+ 1 style sheet
+ 1 graphic file
modernizr-1.5.js

case2

home.htm
slide1.htm
slide2.htm
slide3.htm
slide4.htm
slide5.htm
slide6.htm
+ 1 style sheet
+ 18 graphic files
modernizr-1.5.js

case3

district1.htm
district2.htm
district3.htm
district4.htm
kansas.htm
+ 1 style sheet
+ 2 graphic files
modernizr-1.5.js

case4

cast.htm
commentary.htm
tempest.htm
+ 1 graphic file

Written Communication

Avoiding Common Mistakes in Written Communication

Most written communication errors can be easily avoided, yet are often overlooked. It's particularly important to catch writing errors on a personal Web site or online resume, which often help determing the first impression that a colleague or potential employer forms of you. Whether you are pressed for time, don't pay attention to detail, or have never learned the basics of good writing in the first place, these guidelines should help turn your writing into works you can be proud to claim.

Plan and Focus Your Writing

- Think about your audience. Who will read what you write? What knowledge do they already possess, and what attitudes might they have about your subject? Who will be viewing your Web documents, and what will they expect to see?

- Be clear about why you are writing in the first place. Are you writing to inform, or do you want action to be taken? Do you hope to change a belief or simply state your position? For a personal Web site or resume, make sure you understand what information potential employers and professional contacts will mostly likely be looking for.

- Research your topic. Provide all the necessary information the reader will need to make a decision or take action, if needed. If facts are included, be sure you can substantiate them. For a resume, ensure all your dates are accurate, and look up the exact names of organizations, institutions, and endorsements.

- Don't be afraid to rewrite or revise. If it's an important document, consider having someone else read it so you can determine whether your meaning is clear. At a minimum, read what you have written out loud to determine whether the message and impact come across as you intended. For online documents, continue the revision process on a regular basis so your documents do not become inaccurate or outdated.

Check Grammar and Spelling

Text editing programs remove all excuses for not checking your spelling and grammar in written communications. Keep in mind that spellchecking doesn't catch every error, so be sure to review your work carefully. Hiring managers are often inundated with resumes for a job opening, and an error in spelling or grammar is sometimes all it takes for an otherwise promising application to be rejected.

Set the Right Tone

When you write informal communications, you may use abbreviated or incomplete sentences and phrases or slang. In the workplace, however, you must carefully consider the tone of your written communication so you don't unintentionally offend your readers. Using contractions is considered friendly and is usually all right, but it is never acceptable to use offensive language. Anything you post about yourself online may be viewed by colleagues or a prospective employer, no matter how informal the context, so be sure that anything you write reflects well on you.

ProSkills

Write Clearly and Accessibly

When you write, your language should be free of buzzwords and jargon that will weaken your message, or make it difficult for your reader to understand your meaning.

Create Your Own Web Site

The Web has become an important medium for advertising yourself. By making your resume available online, you can quickly get prospective employers the information they need to make a hiring decision. There are many sites that will assist you in writing and posting your resume. They will also, for a fee, present your online resume to employers in your chosen field. Assuming you don't want to pay to use such a site, you can also create your own Web site containing your employment history and talents. In this exercise, you'll use the skills you learned in Tutorials 1 and 2 to design your own Web site and create an online resume.

Note: Please be sure *not* to include any personal information of a sensitive nature in the documents you create to be submitted to your instructor for this exercise. Later on, you can update the documents with such information for your own personal use.

1. Collect material about yourself that would be useful in an online resume. You should include material for a page on your employment history, talents and special interests, a general biography, and a summary of the main points of your resume.
2. Create a storyboard outlining the pages on your Web site. Clearly indicate the links between the pages. Make sure that your site is easy to navigate no matter which page users start on.
3. Collect or create graphical image files to make your site interesting to viewers. If you obtain graphics from the Web, be sure to follow all copyright restrictions on the material.
4. Start designing your site's home page. It should include an interesting and helpful logo. The home page should be brief and to the point, summarizing the main features of your resume. Its height should not be greater than two screens.
5. Add other pages containing more detailed information. Each page should have a basic theme and topic. The pages should follow a unified theme and design.
6. Use the em and strong elements to highlight important ideas. Do not overuse these page elements; doing so can detract from your page's readability rather than enhancing it.
7. Use numbered and bulleted lists to list the main points in your resume.
8. Use block quotes to highlight recommendations from colleagues and former employers.
9. Use the hr element to divide longer pages into topical sections.
10. If sites on the Web would be relevant to your online resume (such as the Web sites of former or current employers), include links to those sites.
11. Include a link to your e-mail address. Write the e-mail address link so that it automatically adds an appropriate subject line to the e-mail message it creates.
12. Save your completed Web site and present it to your instructor.

Color Names with Color Values, and HTML Character Entities

Both HTML and XHTML allow you to define colors using either color names or color values. HTML and XHTML support a list of 16 basic color names. Most browsers also support an extended list of color names, which are listed in Table A-1 in this appendix, along with their RGB and hexadecimal values. The 16 color names supported by HTML and XHTML appear highlighted in the table. Web-safe colors appear in a bold font.

If you want to use only Web-safe colors, limit your RGB values to 0, 51, 153, 204, and 255 (or limit your hexadecimal values to 00, 33, 66, 99, CC, and FF). For example, an RGB color value of (255, 51, 204) would be Web safe, while an RGB color value of (255, 192, 128) would not.

Table A-2 in this appendix lists the extended character set for HTML, also known as the ISO Latin-1 Character Set. You can specify characters by name or by numeric value. For example, you can use either ® or ® to specify the registered trademark symbol, ®. Not all browsers recognize all code names. Some older browsers that support only the HTML 2.0 standard do not recognize × as a code name, for instance. Code names that older browsers might not recognize are marked with an asterisk in Table A-2.

STARTING DATA FILES

There are no starting Data Files needed for this appendix.

Table A-1:
Color names and corresponding values

Color Name	RGB Value	Hexadecimal Value
aliceblue	(240,248,255)	#F0F8FF
antiquewhite	(250,235,215)	#FAEBD7
aqua	**(0,255,255)**	**#00FFFF**
aquamarine	(127,255,212)	#7FFFD4
azure	(240,255,255)	#F0FFFF
beige	(245,245,220)	#F5F5DC
bisque	(255,228,196)	#FFE4C4
black	**(0,0,0)**	**#000000**
blanchedalmond	(255,235,205)	#FFEBCD
blue	**(0,0,255)**	**#0000FF**
blueviolet	(138,43,226)	#8A2BE2
brown	(165,42,42)	#A52A2A
burlywood	(222,184,135)	#DEB887
cadetblue	(95,158,160)	#5F9EA0
chartreuse	(127,255,0)	#7FFF00
chocolate	(210,105,30)	#D2691E
coral	(255,127,80)	#FF7F50
cornflowerblue	(100,149,237)	#6495ED
cornsilk	(255,248,220)	#FFF8DC
crimson	(220,20,54)	#DC1436
cyan	**(0,255,255)**	**#00FFFF**
darkblue	(0,0,139)	#00008B
darkcyan	(0,139,139)	#008B8B
darkgoldenrod	(184,134,11)	#B8860B
darkgray	(169,169,169)	#A9A9A9
darkgreen	(0,100,0)	#006400
darkkhaki	(189,183,107)	#BDB76B
darkmagenta	(139,0,139)	#8B008B
darkolivegreen	(85,107,47)	#556B2F
darkorange	(255,140,0)	#FF8C00
darkorchid	(153,50,204)	#9932CC
darkred	(139,0,0)	#8B0000
darksalmon	(233,150,122)	#E9967A
darkseagreen	(143,188,143)	#8FBC8F
darkslateblue	(72,61,139)	#483D8B
darkslategray	(47,79,79)	#2F4F4F
darkturquoise	(0,206,209)	#00CED1
darkviolet	(148,0,211)	#9400D3
deeppink	(255,20,147)	#FF1493
deepskyblue	(0,191,255)	#00BFFF
dimgray	(105,105,105)	#696969
dodgerblue	(30,144,255)	#1E90FF
firebrick	(178,34,34)	#B22222
floralwhite	(255,250,240)	#FFFAF0
forestgreen	(34,139,34)	#228B22
fuchsia	**(255,0,255)**	**#FF00FF**

Color Name	RGB Value	Hexadecimal Value
gainsboro	(220,220,220)	#DCDCDC
ghostwhite	(248,248,255)	#F8F8FF
gold	(255,215,0)	#FFD700
goldenrod	(218,165,32)	#DAA520
gray	(128,128,128)	#808080
green	(0,128,0)	#008000
greenyellow	(173,255,47)	#ADFF2F
honeydew	(240,255,240)	#F0FFF0
hotpink	(255,105,180)	#FF69B4
indianred	(205,92,92)	#CD5C5C
indigo	(75,0,130)	#4B0082
ivory	(255,255,240)	#FFFFF0
khaki	(240,230,140)	#F0E68C
lavender	(230,230,250)	#E6E6FA
lavenderblush	(255,240,245)	#FFF0F5
lawngreen	(124,252,0)	#7CFC00
lemonchiffon	(255,250,205)	#FFFACD
lightblue	(173,216,230)	#ADD8E6
lightcoral	(240,128,128)	#F08080
lightcyan	(224,255,255)	#E0FFFF
lightgoldenrodyellow	(250,250,210)	#FAFAD2
lightgreen	(144,238,144)	#90EE90
lightgrey	(211,211,211)	#D3D3D3
lightpink	(255,182,193)	#FFB6C1
lightsalmon	(255,160,122)	#FFA07A
lightseagreen	(32,178,170)	#20B2AA
lightskyblue	(135,206,250)	#87CEFA
lightslategray	(119,136,153)	#778899
lightsteelblue	(176,196,222)	#B0C4DE
lightyellow	(255,255,224)	#FFFFE0
lime	**(0,255,0)**	**#00FF00**
limegreen	(50,205,50)	#32CD32
linen	(250,240,230)	#FAF0E6
magenta	**(255,0,255)**	**#FF00FF**
maroon	(128,0,0)	#800000
mediumaquamarine	(102,205,170)	#66CDAA
mediumblue	(0,0,205)	#0000CD
mediumorchid	(186,85,211)	#BA55D3
mediumpurple	(147,112,219)	#9370DB
mediumseagreen	(60,179,113)	#3CB371
mediumslateblue	(123,104,238)	#7B68EE
mediumspringgreen	(0,250,154)	#00FA9A
mediumturquoise	(72,209,204)	#48D1CC
mediumvioletred	(199,21,133)	#C71585
midnightblue	(25,25,112)	#191970
mintcream	(245,255,250)	#F5FFFA
mistyrose	(255,228,225)	#FFE4E1

Color Name	RGB Value	Hexadecimal Value
moccasin	(255,228,181)	#FFE4B5
navajowhite	(255,222,173)	#FFDEAD
navy	**(0,0,128)**	#000080
oldlace	(253,245,230)	#FDF5E6
olive	(128,128,0)	#808000
olivedrab	(107,142,35)	#6B8E23
orange	(255,165,0)	#FFA500
orangered	(255,69,0)	#FF4500
orchid	(218,112,214)	#DA70D6
palegoldenrod	(238,232,170)	#EEE8AA
palegreen	(152,251,152)	#98FB98
paleturquoise	(175,238,238)	#AFEEEE
palevioletred	(219,112,147)	#DB7093
papayawhip	(255,239,213)	#FFEFD5
peachpuff	(255,218,185)	#FFDAB9
peru	(205,133,63)	#CD853F
pink	(255,192,203)	#FFC0CB
plum	(221,160,221)	#DDA0DD
powderblue	(176,224,230)	#B0E0E6
purple	**(128,0,128)**	#808080
red	**(255,0,0)**	#FF0000
rosybrown	(188,143,143)	#BC8F8F
royalblue	(65,105,0)	#4169E1
saddlebrown	(139,69,19)	#8B4513
salmon	(250,128,114)	#FA8072
sandybrown	(244,164,96)	#F4A460
seagreen	(46,139,87)	#2E8B57
seashell	(255,245,238)	#FFF5EE
sienna	(160,82,45)	#A0522D
silver	(192,192,192)	#C0C0C0
skyblue	(135,206,235)	#87CEEB
slateblue	(106,90,205)	#6A5ACD
slategray	(112,128,144)	#708090
snow	(255,250,250)	#FFFAFA
springgreen	(0,255,127)	#00FF7F
steelblue	(70,130,180)	#4682B4
tan	(210,180,140)	#D2B48C
teal	(0,128,128)	#008080
thistle	(216,191,216)	#D8BFD8
tomato	(255,99,71)	#FF6347
turquoise	(64,224,208)	#40E0D0
violet	(238,130,238)	#EE82EE
wheat	(245,222,179)	#F5DEB3
white	**(255,255,255)**	#FFFFFF
whitesmoke	(245,245,245)	#F5F5F5
yellow	**(255,255,0)**	#FFFF00
yellowgreen	(154,205,50)	#9ACD32

Character	Code	Code Name	Description
	`&#09;`		Tab
	`&#10;`		Line feed
	`&#32;`		Space
!	`&#33;`		Exclamation mark
"	`&#34;`	`&quot;`	Double quotation mark
#	`&#35;`		Pound sign
$	`&#36;`		Dollar sign
%	`&#37;`		Percent sign
&	`&#38;`	`&amp;`	Ampersand
'	`&#39;`		Apostrophe
(	`&#40;`		Left parenthesis
)	`&#41;`		Right parenthesis
*	`&#42;`		Asterisk
+	`&#43;`		Plus sign
,	`&#44;`		Comma
-	`&#45;`		Hyphen
.	`&#46;`		Period
/	`&#47;`		Forward slash
0 - 9	`&#48;–&#57;`		Numbers 0–9
:	`&#58;`		Colon
;	`&#59;`		Semicolon
<	`&#60;`	`&lt;`	Less than sign
=	`&#61;`		Equal sign
>	`&#62;`	`&gt;`	Greater than sign
?	`&#63;`		Question mark
@	`&#64;`		Commercial at sign
A - Z	`&#65;–&#90;`		Letters A–Z
[	`&#91;`		Left square bracket
\	`&#92;`		Back slash
]	`&#93;`		Right square bracket
^	`&#94;`		Caret
_	`&#95;`		Horizontal bar (underscore)
`	`&#96;`		Grave accent
a - z	`&#97;–&#122;`		Letters a–z
{	`&#123;`		Left curly brace
|	`&#124;`		Vertical bar
}	`&#125;`		Right curly brace
~	`&#126;`		Tilde
‚	`&#130;`		Comma
ƒ	`&#131;`		Function sign (florin)
„	`&#132;`		Double quotation mark
…	`&#133;`		Ellipsis
†	`&#134;`		Dagger

Character	Code	Code Name	Description
‡	&#135;		Double dagger
ˆ	&#136;		Circumflex
‰	&#137;		Permil
Š	&#138;		Capital S with hacek
‹	&#139;		Left single angle
Œ	&#140;		Capital OE ligature
	–		Unused
'	&#145;		Single beginning quotation mark
'	&#146;		Single ending quotation mark
"	&#147;		Double beginning quotation mark
"	&#148;		Double ending quotation mark
•	&#149;		Bullet
–	&#150;		En dash
—	&#151;		Em dash
~	&#152;		Tilde
™	&#153;	™*	Trademark symbol
š	&#154;		Small s with hacek
›	&#155;		Right single angle
œ	&#156;		Lowercase oe ligature
Ÿ	&#159;		Capital Y with umlaut
		*	Non-breaking space
¡	&#161;	¡*	Inverted exclamation mark
¢	&#162;	¢*	Cent sign
£	&#163;	£*	Pound sterling
¤	&#164;	¤*	General currency symbol
¥	&#165;	¥*	Yen sign
¦	&#166;	¦*	Broken vertical bar
§	&#167;	§*	Section sign
¨	&#168;	¨*	Umlaut
©	&#169;	©*	Copyright symbol
ª	&#170;	ª*	Feminine ordinal
«	&#171;	«*	Left angle quotation mark
¬	&#172;	¬*	Not sign
	&#173;	­*	Soft hyphen
®	&#174;	®*	Registered trademark
¯	&#175;	¯*	Macron
°	&#176;	°*	Degree sign
±	&#177;	±*	Plus/minus symbol
2	&#178;	²*	Superscript 2
3	&#179;	³*	Superscript 3
´	&#180;	´*	Acute accent
µ	&#181;	µ*	Micro sign
¶	&#182;	¶*	Paragraph sign

Character	Code	Code Name	Description
·	&#183;	·*	Middle dot
ç	&#184;	¸*	Cedilla
1	&#185;	¹*	Superscript 1
º	&#186;	º*	Masculine ordinal
»	&#187;	»*	Right angle quotation mark
¼	&#188;	¼*	Fraction one-quarter
½	&#189;	½*	Fraction one-half
¾	&#190;	¾*	Fraction three-quarters
¿	&#191;	¿*	Inverted question mark
À	&#192;	&Agrave;	Capital A, grave accent
Á	&#193;	&Aacute;	Capital A, acute accent
Â	&#194;	&Acirc;	Capital A, circumflex accent
Ã	&#195;	&Atilde;	Capital A, tilde
Ä	&#196;	&Auml;	Capital A, umlaut
Å	&#197;	&Aring;	Capital A, ring
Æ	&#198;	&Aelig;	Capital AE ligature
Ç	&#199;	&Ccedil;	Capital C, cedilla
È	&#200;	&Egrave;	Capital E, grave accent
É	&#201;	&Eacute;	Capital E, acute accent
Ê	&#202;	&Ecirc;	Capital E, circumflex accent
Ë	&#203;	&Euml;	Capital E, umlaut
Ì	&#204;	&Igrave;	Capital I, grave accent
Í	&#205;	&Iacute;	Capital I, acute accent
Î	&#206;	&Icirc;	Capital I, circumflex accent
Ï	&#207;	&Iuml;	Capital I, umlaut
Ð	&#208;	Ð*	Capital ETH, Icelandic
Ñ	&#209;	&Ntilde;	Capital N, tilde
Ò	&#210;	&Ograve;	Capital O, grave accent
Ó	&#211;	&Oacute;	Capital O, acute accent
Ô	&#212;	&Ocirc;	Capital O, circumflex accent
Õ	&#213;	&Otilde;	Capital O, tilde
Ö	&#214;	&Ouml;	Capital O, umlaut
×	&#215;	×*	Multiplication sign
Ø	&#216;	&Oslash;	Capital O slash
Ù	&#217;	&Ugrave;	Capital U, grave accent
Ú	&#218;	&Uacute;	Capital U, acute accent
Û	&#219;	&Ucirc;	Capital U, circumflex accent
Ü	&#220;	&Uuml;	Capital U, umlaut
Ý	&#221;	&Yacute;	Capital Y, acute accent
Þ	&#222;	&THORN;	Capital THORN, Icelandic
ß	&#223;	&szlig;	Small sz ligature
à	&#224;	&agrave;	Small a, grave accent
á	&#225;	&aacute;	Small a, acute accent

Character	Code	Code Name	Description
â	â	â	Small a, circumflex accent
ã	ã	ã	Small a, tilde
ä	ä	ä	Small a, umlaut
å	å	å	Small a, ring
æ	æ	æ	Small ae ligature
ç	ç	ç	Small c, cedilla
è	è	è	Small e, grave accent
é	é	é	Small e, acute accent
ê	ê	ê	Small e, circumflex accent
ë	ë	ë	Small e, umlaut
ì	ì	ì	Small i, grave accent
í	í	í	Small i, acute accent
î	î	î	Small i, circumflex accent
ï	ï	ï	Small i, umlaut
ð	ð	ð	Small eth, Icelandic
ñ	ñ	ñ	Small n, tilde
ò	ò	ò	Small o, grave accent
ó	ó	ó	Small o, acute accent
ô	ô	ô	Small o, circumflex accent
õ	õ	õ	Small o, tilde
ö	ö	ö	Small o, umlaut
÷	÷	÷*	Division sign
ø	ø	ø	Small o slash
ù	ù	ù	Small u, grave accent
ú	ú	ú	Small u, acute accent
û	û	û	Small u, circumflex accent
ü	ü	ü	Small u, umlaut
ý	ý	ý	Small y, acute accent
þ	þ	þ	Small thorn, Icelandic
ÿ	ÿ	ÿ	Small y, umlaut

GLOSSARY/INDEX

URL. *See* Uniform Resource Locator

UTF-8 The commonly used character set on the Web stored as a compressed version of Unicode. HTML 54

V

validator Program that examines document code to ensure that it meets all the syntax requirements of the specified language. HTML 11

var element, HTML 45

W

WAN. *See* wide area network

W3C. *See* World Wide Web Consortium

Web. *See* World Wide Web

Web browser A device or program that retrieves the page from its Web server and renders it on a computer or another device. HTML 5

Web Hypertext Application Technology Working Group (WHATWG) A group of Web designers and browser manufacturers formed with the mission to develop a rival version to XHTML 2.0, called HTML5. HTML 6

Web page A document on the World Wide Web. HTML 5

Web server A server storing a Web page. HTML 5

Web site
    linking to, HTML 110–114
    management, HTML 89

Web site structure, HTML 74–79
    hierarchical, HTML 76
    linear, HTML 75
    mixed, HTML 76–78
    protected, HTML 78–79

WHATWG. *See* Web Hypertext Application Technology Working Group

white space The blank spaces, tabs, and line breaks found within a text file. HTML 9–10

wide area network (WAN) A network that covers a wider area, such as several buildings or cities, typically consisting of two or more local area networks. HTML 4

window, secondary, opening, HTML 117–119

World Wide Web A graphical interface to the Internet using hypertext links as a mean to access interconnected documents and services. HTML 4
    history, HTML 4–5

World Wide Web Consortium (W3C) An organization of Web designers and programmers that creates a set of standards or specifications for all browser manufacturers to follow. HTML 5

X

XHTML. *See* Extensible Hypertext Markup Language

XHTML 2.0 An aborted version of XHTML, created to provide robust support for multimedia, social networking, interactive Web forms, and other features needed by Web designers. HTML 6

XML. *See* Extensible Markup Language

XML vocabulary Markup language developed using XML. HTML 6